Navajo Ceremonial Baskets

Sacred Symbols
Sacred Space

Georgiana Kennedy Simpson

Native Voices
Summertown, Tennessee

Cover design by Warren Jefferson
Book design by Jerry Lee Hutchens
Interior photographs are by Georgiana Kennedy Simpson, unless otherwise noted.
Cover photo: Bruce Hucko took this beautiful photograph of Valentina S. Smith, a 16 year-old honor student from Monument Valley High School. She says, "When I put on my Navajo dress and hold the basket, it's like going back in time to how my great-grandparents lived. Their lives help make me strong."

Native Voices

Book Publishing Company
P. O. Box 99
Summertown, TN 38483

04 03 02 01 4 3 2 1

ISBN 1-57067-118-4

Simpson, Georgiana Kennedy.
  Navajo ceremonial baskets : sacred symbols, sacred space / Georgiana Kennedy Simpson.
      p. cm.
Includes index.
  ISBN 1-57067-118-4
  1. Navajo baskets--History. 2. Navajo Indians--Rites and ceremonies. 3. Navajo weavers. I. Title.
  E99.N3S56 2003
  746.41'20899726--dc22

                              2003025512

Table of Contents

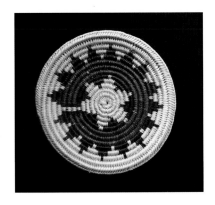

Basket woven by Rose Ann Whiskers.

To my father—

who instilled in me a love of the Southwest.

To my mother—

who demonstrated how beauty and art feed the soul.

To my Grandmother Kennedy—

in whose memory I drew the courage to write.

The boys and girls that are growing now, they're going to learn this and if they understand this, they will learn it in school, they will take care of it for themselves and into the future as they grow. They will carry it on . . . they won't erase it . . . they will learn it and they will have a good life. I don't want it to be erased. I want it to be carried on from generation to generation. It's a very valuable subject that I am telling you. There are all different ways to talk about it.

—June Blackhorse, Navajo Medicine Man

Special Dedication

Sadly, two weeks after our final interview, June Blackhorse passed away. Fittingly, he was performing a sacred ceremony at the time of his death. In the words of my friend, Jerry Hutchens, "He died in the harness." A couple of months prior to his passing, June had heart surgery and, despite his failing health, had continued to perform ceremonies.

When the younger people reflected on June's behavior that night they remembered that he had reminded them that the ceremonies and traditions will not die when he dies. He told them that if they are strong, the traditions and ceremonies will live on in each of them. He had just finished singing a ceremonial song and was in the middle of the second one when he passed from the Glittering World.

June's generosity with me through the course of our discussions cannot be overemphasized. He patiently fielded mundane, and what at times must have seemed inane, questions from me. In spite of this, he handled every discussion with respect and understanding. It's not that June did not have a sense of humor, in fact, he was well known for his teasing. Interpreters were needed for each of our sessions and June took these opportunities to educate the younger people in the traditional ways of the Navajo. Detailed answers were given to every question, and he went to great lengths to ensure that I understood his responses. At the end of our last session, he expressed a desire to move beyond this project and record his knowledge of the clans. Unfortunately we did not have the time.

In the Navajo way, you say "thank you" at the end of your conversation. June always thanked me for asking him questions and for recording the information for the Navajo children. I always thanked him for his generosity and candor. He will not see this book. His children and grandchildren will, however, and ultimately that was June's wish.

Georgiana Kennedy Simpson
April 30, 2003

Acknowledgements

I have given birth to two children and have compared the writing of this book to a four year pregnancy. Many of you may be able to relate to the mixed feelings. My editor was thinking, "Is it here yet?" while my husband's thoughts leaned more toward, "Is this ever going to end?" Fortunately for both, after much labor, some excruciating, mostly delightful, I have once again "delivered the goods."

This book is not just about a basket, it is about people and their thoughts. The idea was hatched in discussions between John and Jacque Foutz, owners of the best private collection of historic Navajo baskets, and the Simpson family, owners of the best contemporary Navajo basket collection. These two collections represent a plethora of designs and a corresponding dearth of information relating to the origin and meaning of Navajo baskets. In my research, by and large, people with whom I met were generous with their expertise. The story of the ceremonial basket is shared from many different perspectives, a culmination of knowledge deposited in the minds of medicine men, weavers, cultural teachers, traders and academics, both present and past. My way of thanking these individuals is to pass along their teachings in the pages of this book. I must, too, recognize my Navajo interpreters, Allison Billy, Natalie Nez, Priscilla Sagg, and Amelia Yellowman. The teachings from June Blackhorse and John Holiday would have been impossible without you. Natalie, an extra thanks to you for a thousand-and-one digital downloads.

I am especially indebted to several scholars who provided guidance through the trickiest chapter for me, History and Archaeology of Navajo Baskets. From the Museum of Indian Art and Culture/Laboratory of Anthropology, I owe special thanks to John Torres, Curator of Archaeology; Valerie Verzuh, Collections Manager; and Laura Holt, Librarian (retired). Each one's specific brand of knowledge opened a door to exploring the relationship between contemporary and historic baskets. Jim Copeland, Bureau of Land Management Archaeologist, beyond sharing his love of Navajo archaeology, was helpful when images specific to Dinétah were needed. He also guided me to rare examples of Navajo archaeological basket materials. For my editor, Jerry Hutchens, God has reserved a special place in heaven for you. Last time we collaborated, I likened the experience to herding cats, since Jerry had to coordinate five authors, including me. I think, this time, Jerry's experience was similar with the notable exception of the multiple felines dwelling in the tangled recesses of my brain. Thank you for your faith and patience.

Kira and Grange, my two beautiful redheaded children—you both inspire me every day and our love carries me through the most difficult of times. Finally, to my husband, Steve, my thanks to you for reading and commenting on numerous rewrites. Your technical writing skills provided polish to the spinning processes of my creative mind. I love you.

Navajo people often refer to the relationship of their many ceremonial ways as the branches of a tree which extend over every occasion, bearing and protecting the Navajo way of life. They identify Blessingway as the trunk of this tree which supports all other ceremonial branches. This tree stands deep rooted in the creation of the world.

—Sam Gill, author of Native American Religious Action:
A Performance Approach to Religion

Tree basket woven by Elsie Holiday.
—Courtesy Simpson Family Collection.

1. The Origin of Navajo Ceremony

With over fifty years of collective experience in working with Navajo baskets, my brother-in-law, Barry, my husband, Steve, and I realized that even with all our experience, we knew little about the origin and usage of Navajo ceremonial baskets. Armed with two sketchy stories describing the design itself, I embarked on a journey that has taken me deep into Navajo history and far across the southwestern landscape. The result is a translation of stories by those most intimately involved with the ceremonial basket: the medicine people and their patients who use the basket; the weavers who create the basket; the other teachers of Navajo culture (in addition to the medicine people); and the traders who supply baskets for ceremonies as well as a place for safekeeping when the baskets are not in use.

When my husband first moved back to Utah, he immersed himself in reading the history of the Navajo people. Formally, trained as a lawyer, he soon found himself frustrated by contradictions in the traditional stories. In later years, he has come to realize that stories arising from an oral tradition have much to do with the personal experiences of the person relating the story—whether it is Hasteen Klah passing along his rich experience to Franc Johnson Newcomb and Mary Cabot Wheelwright, or basket artist Mary Holiday Black teaching her daughter, Lorraine.

Mary Black instructing her daughter Lorraine.

Rather than see thought as derivative of ritual practice, we should begin with thought. That is where the Navajo stories begin and that is where they tell us to begin. I think we should pay attention. Everything begins with thought. The world that we live in began with thought. The songs that put the hogan in place were sung after the people emerged from the earth. In building a hogan this process of creating the Navajo world is continued. The songs are about building a house, but they are at the same time about building the world. The mountains are put in place, the plants, the moisture, everything. And as you place each and every part of the house and the world you sing "he was thinking about it," he was thinking about placing this particular mountain, this particular support post for my house and for the sky, the plants, the moisture, everything. (Farella 1995, xxviii-xxix)

Coyote talks about this in great detail. He describes all the differences and oppositions that occur in the world. On the one hand he argues that they are necessary if life is to be the way that people want it; but he is also arguing or pointing out something else. He is saying that these differences exist, they are existential, so we might as well accept that and get used to it. One of the big things in this world view is accepting the givens of existence, not fighting against them.

And Coyote is talking about this and arguing it to the other diyinii (Diyin Dene'é). And they are listening but they all have different opinions on what he is saying. Which also tells you something. So he says well let's take a

Tools and materials for making baskets.

vote then. He asks, should we think in one way only or should different ways of thinking be allowed? They vote and half of them want to allow only one way of thinking, and the other half want to allow difference.

Coyote says, even on this simple thing you can't agree. You even disagree, think differently, about the existence of difference. (Farella, 1995, xl)

The experiences conveyed in the following stories may, at first, seem widely disparate. The medicine people themselves understand that other Navajo people may have a different way of explaining the history, structure, and use of the basket, and that difference lies in each person's path to traditional knowledge. Despite the differences found in various texts and translations, what is more remarkable are the consistencies that exist throughout the various stories and translations. In this volume, the seemingly simple design of the basket will unfold into a visual metaphor of the landscape. Each basket chosen for use in a ceremony represents the personal history of the patient while serving as a reminder to all people present of who they are and from where they come. Hopefully, upon reading this story, you will come to the same understanding I reached—the basket serves as a powerful visual metaphor of a Navajo person's life; it conveys the history of the Navajo people; and it symbolizes the land that they call home, Dinétah.

We cannot speak of the ceremonial basket without first speaking of Navajo ceremony. Ceremony is defined as a set of acts performed as prescribed by custom, ritual, or etiquette. Gladys Reichard tries to demonstrate this principle in her wonderful writing, *Navajo Religion: A Study of Symbolism.* Reichard believed that there is much more to the dance, song, and sandpainting than the primitiveness that meets the casual eye. There is a religious system that for years has enabled the Navajo to retain their identity in a rapidly changing world.

> A Navaho ceremony, whatever it may be called, is a combination of many elements—ritualistic items such as the medicine bundle (jish) with its sacred contents; prayersticks, made of carefully selected wood and feathers, precious stones, tobacco, water collected from sacred places, a tiny piece of cotton string; song, with its lyrical and musical complexities; sandpaintings, with intricate color, directional, and impressionistic symbols; prayer, with stress on order and rhythmic unity; plants, with supernatural qualities defined and personified; body and figure painting; sweating and emetic, with purificatory functions; vigil, with emphasis on concentration and summary. But it is the selection of these and other elements and their orderly combination into a unit that makes the chant or ceremony effective. (Reichard, 1950)

So where does ceremony begin? For the Navajo people, the origin of their ceremonies can be traced to the earliest stories. In the Emergence Myth, as told by Gishin Begay to Father Berard Haile in 1908, the legend of the people's journey from the first world to the present world is related. In the story different beings are introduced as they progress through each level. Explanations for the existence of evil and other scourges and the ceremonies put in place to overcome these difficulties are folded into each stage.

Washington Matthews (1843-1905) was one of the earliest Anglo recorders of Navajo culture. The origin of ceremony is laid out in Washington Matthews' account of The Visionary (Bił áhát'íinii) who lived at Tséyi, a classic tale of the hero's transformation. In an interview with journalist Bill Moyers, Joseph Campbell states, "The hero is someone who has given his life to something bigger than himself or other than himself. . . There is a big transformation of consciousness that's concerned. And what all the myths have to deal with is the transformation of consciousness—that you're thinking in *this* way, and you have now to think in *that* way." This legend provides the instruction of how medicine ways came to the Navajo people through the journeys and lessons of The Visionary. The third of four brothers, The Visionary saw strange things

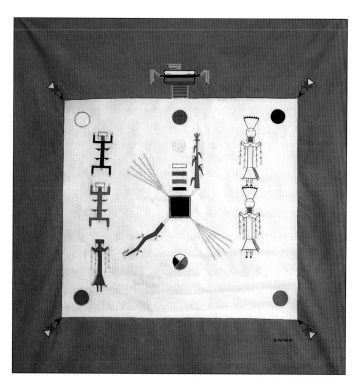

Very early sandpainting belonging to the Emergence Myth. The top center circle represents a basket of sacred pollen. Painting by Dennis Hathale.
—Courtesy of Georgiana Kennedy Simpson Private Collection.

and heard strange songs while out on solitary walks. His brothers did not believe him, and ignored him when he tried to teach them the songs he had heard.

One day, his brothers and a brother-in-law went out on a hunt while Bił áhát'íinii stayed behind. He later set out after them. On his way, he encountered Crow People and came to realize his brothers would be unable to kill more deer because they mistakenly killed a magpie and a crow. When he finally caught up with the hunting party, he related his story and was scorned by everyone except the brother-in-law, who was beginning to recognize the talents of their little brother. Over the next four days, the brothers were unsuccessful in their deer hunt. As a result of their hunting failure, and with a dawning realization that their brother was correct in his interpretation, they decided to return home. On the way, they encountered four Rocky Mountain sheep. The elder brother asked The Visionary to head them off and shoot them. Four times the mountain sheep approached and four times their little brother found himself unable to shoot them. After the fourth try, the sheep threw off their masks and revealed themselves as the holy ones, Bigháá' ask'idii, the Humpback Gods.

The four Bighą́ą́' ask'idii approached The Visionary with a skin and mask and asked him to join them. When one of the brothers finally came looking for him, he saw The Visionary's clothing and weapons. His footprints disappeared, and a fifth bighorn's tracks appeared. The brother observed that each sheep had taken four steps to reach the edge of the precipice. Upon descending into the canyon, which was terraced, he noticed the tracks of five sheep, each sheep taking four steps; but beyond the fourth terrace no footprints could be found. Upon ascending out of the canyon, he decided to leave the clothes where they lay, and upon joining the others, he related what he had observed.

> "Now," said the brother-in-law, "What do you think? How do you account for the strange things that have happened? You would not believe what our brother told you, but his words have all come true. Now one of our brothers is lost to us." "True," said the eldest brother,

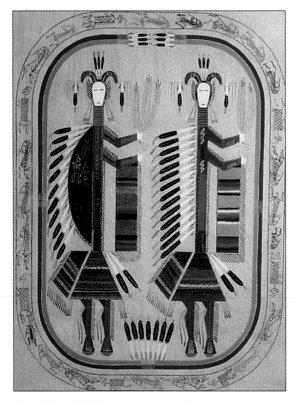

Bighą́ą́' ask'idii, (Humpback) on left side, represented in contemporary sandpainting by Navajo Artist, Cecil Myerson.
—Courtesy of Twin Rocks Trading Post.

"I did not believe what my brother said; but I believe it now." (Matthews 1995, 663)

Upon returning to their home, they put turquoise, white shell, haliotis shell, and cannel coal into one sacred basket. Into another basket, they put specular iron-ore, blue pollen, life pollen, and corn pollen, singing as they did this. They took these things back to where the clothes lay. The second brother laid the baskets on the edge of the cliff where the tracks ended, and repeated the prayer to Talking God. He then prayed to all the other gods, to whom all Navajo people now pray in the rite of the Night Chant. When they were finished praying, Wind whispered to them and said, "Do the things I bid you and on the fourth day after this, early in the morning, your brother will return to you." Then they all went home.

The story goes on from here and describes the return of Bił áhát'íinii and the subsequent teaching of his experiences.

He said: "For a long time you have not believed my words; but now you know that some things I told you were true. When you were out hunting I foretold that which came to pass." Then he told the story of his pursuit of the bighorns and went on from there. When he and the four Ga'naskidi (Bighą́ą́' ask'idii) jumped from the edge of the canyon, where the hunters last saw their tracks, they alighted on a very narrow ledge which ran along the face of the canyon wall and they followed this ledge until they came to a place where they met Talking God, Hastseyalti (Haashch'éélti'í— Talking God), and the House God, Hastse'hooghan (Áłtsé Hooghan). These gods sent word to other Yé'ii that they had with them a mortal man whom they were bringing home, and soon they met a multitude of the Ye'idine' (Yé'ii dine'é), the Holy people, which gathered around the prophet and gazed at him. Assembled were the twelve chiefs of the gods who had sent the younger Ga'naskidi (Bighą́ą́' ask'idii) to capture the prophet; plus many holy ones of lesser degree. Many divine animals and birds were in the throng; among these he saw Coyote, Bluebirds, and Yellow Birds. When he arrived at the home of the yé'ii he observed that they were preparing sacred objects and conducting rites and he said: "I desire to learn your rites and I will give you twelve large buckskins if you teach me." They said they would do this, and it was thus he came to learn the ceremony. (Matthews 1902, 164-165, 667)

Navajo medicine man, John Holiday.

Before the earth was created as we know it now, there were the jewel baskets—one of white shell, one of turquoise, one of jet, one of abalone, and two others. When First Man and First Woman were created, then the regular ceremonial basket came after these baskets. This ceremonial basket is all of the jewel baskets combined into one.

John Holiday
Monument Valley, Utah, April 16, 2001

2. The Origin of Ceremonial Baskets

The origin of the ceremonial basket reaches back into the deepest parts of Navajo history. The basket's place is firmly embedded in the first stories of the people and their gods. In order to understand the basket's importance in ceremonial and everyday life, we turn to these stories to understand its role in providing a sacred, protected space while giving visual instruction about one's life and the history of the Navajo people.

The Jewel Baskets

The jewel baskets are the foundation of all ceremonial baskets throughout Navajo history. In order to understand the origin of the ceremonial baskets, we journey back to the origins of the Navajo people, back to the First World. (Depending on the reference, we currently reside in either the Fourth or Fifth World.) We look again to the story of The Visionary (Bił áhát'íinii) for guidance and insight into the genesis of the jewel baskets. After descending into the canyon with the Bighą́ą́'ask'idíí, the Bighorn Sheep, our hero is taught ceremonies by the yé'ii, or holy ones.

Contemporary interpretation of jewel baskets by Peggy Black.
—Courtesy of Simpson Family Collection.

Now the yé'ii sent out messengers to bring in the sacrifices which the
brothers had laid on the brink of the canyon. Out of the inkli'z (nitł'iz), the
precious stones and shells left in the baskets by the brothers of Bitahatini
(Bił áhát'íinii), they made five great bowls or baskets: a basket of turquoise,
a basket of white shell, a basket of haliotis shell, a basket of cannel coal, and
a basket of rock crystal. They had the power to take a small fragment and
make it grow to any size and shape they wished. Then they put a sacred
buckskin over each basket; they prayed and sang over them and jumped
over each in four different directions. The prophet sat by and watched carefully all these rites and remembered them. One old yé'ii taught him the
songs and he learned them more readily than any man has learned them
since. The yé'ii made in his presence the masks and sang over them the
songs of Hozo'ndze (Hózhǫ́ǫ́jí). (Matthews, 165)

The many references to these special baskets provide a connection to the
sacred and important role baskets play in the overall scheme of Navajo life. They
were created by the gods. They are carried by the gods. They are treated with

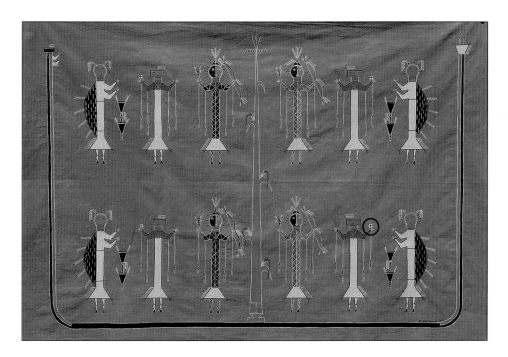

Dennis Hathale memory aid showing the four goddess figures holding jewel baskets. One of the jewel baskets is circled for identification. Also shown are four Humpback gods and two Fringe Mouth of the Water and two Fringe Mouth of the Land, each face wreathed with a cloud headdress.
—Georgiana Kennedy Simpson Private Collection.

respect according to guidelines laid out by the gods. More importantly, these baskets provide a symbol for order and clarity within the Navajo mind as well as a means of organizing the surrounding external environment.

The Diyin Dine'é combined their "mysterious powers and colors" to create the first sacred baskets from the fundamental living elements. Each individual basket was identified and named according to the material from which it was constructed.

> Black Jet Basket, Turquoise Basket, Abalone Shell Basket, and White Shell Basket. This is the reason why there are black, blue, yellow, red, and white colors in the basket. Sometimes you can only see black and red. . . The Holy People blessed it [the basket] with good thoughts, ideas, thinking, and planning. . . The purpose of why this basket was made was to create and keep all creation in order. To keep the directions, thoughts, ideas, thinking, and planning in order. To keep nature, the Holy People's laws in order, so they won't be confusing. So there could be East, South, West, North, and Spring, Summer, Fall, and Winter. When the Holy People wanted life to

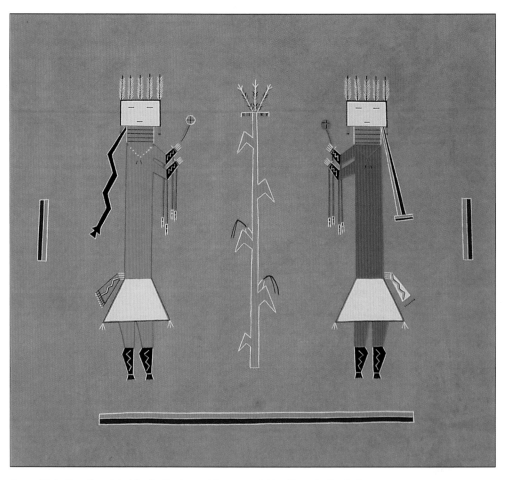

Long Hair People with Magic Baskets. Memory aid by Dennis Hathale.

exist, they used this basket to put their children together, to produce life. (Schwarz 1997, 39)

References to the original baskets arise time and again in the early stories of the Navajo people, and in their visual cues, the sandpaintings. For example, in the sandpainting from the eighth day of the night chant, there are four goddess figures, each represented with a bunch of spruce twigs in one hand and a sacred jeweled basket in the other. These jewel or magic baskets provided a means of transport for the gods, allowing them to travel great distances at great speeds along a rainbow (nááts'íílid) path.

A story in the Water Chant tells of a young man who entices the holy maidens of the Hopi People (Kiis'áanii) by changing his form. For good reason, the Kiis'áanii were quite angry with the young man and they planned to punish the girls for leaving with him. An old woman came to warn them, however, and then another woman appeared and brought them a white shell basket. She gave it to the older of the two girls saying that this basket would help them escape.

> Then the Holy People put the white shell basket down on the ground and the girls got into it, the older one leading. The Youth sat at the side holding a feather prayerstick in each hand, and he gave the Tsin-tralth (tsihał—feather prayerstick) to the older girl and Tchoh-ranh (ch'ó) to the younger. The four Diginnih (Diyin Dine'é) or Holy People stood around them, one east, one south, one west, and one north, and they placed a rainbow (nááts' íílid) under the basket from the west to the east, and lightning from the north to the south, and it began to rise from the earth, but only lifted a little and then sank to earth again. Suddenly Dontso appeared and said to them, "You should have told your grandfather, Hashje-alchee, (Haashch'ééłchíí') the Red Hashje-altye, that you wanted to go up into the sky." (B'Gohdi, Klah 1933, 61-62)

The young man experiences many more adventures with his ultimate goal of locating his "dream girl." After these adventures, the young man finds and marries the girl of his dreams. His wife's father tells him of more medicine ways, and then the old man asks to have a ceremony.

> The Youth agreed to give the ceremony over his father-in-law, and asked the rest of the family to go out and get medicine for him, and they brought in herbs for emetics and prepared them. The old man asked how many baskets were needed and the Youth said five—of jet, turquoise, abalone, white shell, and red shell. (Klah 1933, 76)

A Different Beginning

Conversations with the medicine men, teachers of Navajo culture, weavers, and other Navajo people not only were the most enjoyable events in searching for the ceremonial basket's story, but they continuously drove home the point how personal each individual's background and teaching are and how their experiences shape their understanding of the basket and its origins. One day, when talking to Betty Yazzie, our local senior citizens coordinator, she related her relationship with the basket. Before Betty worked in her current position, she spent several years as the Navajo culture instructor at the Rough Rock Demonstration School. Betty learned to make baskets when she was twenty-one. At that time, she was married to a Ute man and watched her mother-in-law make baskets. She tried making one on her own. Her first basket came out rough and ugly, so she tossed it aside. Her mother-in-law saw the basket and told her not to do it that way and that she would teach Betty how to make a proper basket. Betty's paternal grandfather once related to her how the Navajo people came to have the basket. He said the Ute and Navajo people were warring against each other. They wanted to make peace. The Ute said, "We will give you this basket to use in your ceremonies and for you to know that we are at peace with you." In return, the Navajo people gave the Ute something, although Betty could not recall what that was.

June Blackhorse, a respected medicine man from the local area relates this story in a different way. He tells the story of Kicking Rock Man (Rock-Putting-It-Back-Again-Man). He lived at the edge of a cliff, and his children lived beneath the ledge. If a person passed, he would kick them off the ledge to feed his children. When Monster Slayer (Naayéé' Neezghání) was helping rid the Navajo people of the monsters that terrorized them, he killed Kicking Rock Man and kicked him over the ledge to his own children. The children cried and told Monster Slayer that they did not wish to eat their own father and that they wished to live. So, bargaining with the Hero Twins (Born-for-Water [Tó bájíshchíní] as well as Monster Slayer), they told Monster Slayer how to find the gift that will save their lives. They begged Monster Slayer, "Tomorrow, come back tomorrow . . . one to two miles from where we are and we will have something for you." So, that first day, Monster Slayer returned and walked toward the south where he found a small basket with no design. On the second day, Monster Slayer walked toward the sunrise where he saw them working on the basket and the basket was showing the first design elements. As Kicking Rock Man's children were travelling, they were gathering sumac (chiiłchin) and working as a team to create the basket. The third day, he walked a couple miles toward the north to find a basket with the rainbow element represented. Finally, on the fourth day, Monster Slayer walked a couple of miles toward the sun and found the completed basket. At this point, June leans in and says, "The Ute people at Towaoc (Colorado) . . . they are the descendants of Kicking Rock Man." (A similar version of this story is told in Raymond Friday Locke's volume, *The Book of the Navajo*. It does not include the basket making portion of the story, and it says the one surviving child of Kicking Rock Man is the progenitor of the Paiute people.)

One day, my brother-in-law, Barry Simpson, was bantering with a respected Ute basket weaver, Susan Whyte (1934-1994) about the origin of the ceremonial basket.

Her response was, "You crazy white man. It was the Ute people who came up with that design." Her response makes a lot of sense because the Navajo people indeed relied heavily on surrounding Ute and Paiute weavers to provide a majority of baskets for ceremonies over the years. It is well documented how numerous taboos existed that prescribed when a woman could and could not weave. Some felt these taboos became so cumbersome that it was almost impossible for a Navajo weaver to complete a basket. What is more telling are the economic conditions that existed throughout the 1900s, a pure example of supply-and-demand market dynamics. Simply put, with the large population of the Navajo Nation and constant demand for baskets to be used ceremonially, it was virtually impossible for Navajo weavers to keep up with the supply. June Blackhorse is explicit in stating that the Utes have no ceremonial need for the baskets—they were simply woven for Navajo use.

Who Wove the First Basket?

Changing Woman (Asdzą́ą́ Nádleehé), so named because she renews her youth as the seasons progress, was created and trained to bring forth sons who freed the earth from the monsters. Old, gray-haired, wrinkled, and bent in the winter, she gradually transforms herself into a young and beautiful woman. Restoration to youth is the pattern of the earth, something for which the Navajo lives, for he reasons that what happens to the earth may also happen to him. Regaining strength after disease due to contact with strangers, attack by evil or offended powers, or loss of ritualistic purity is interpreted as rejuvenation like that of Mother Earth.

Gladys Reichard

Navajo people raised with any knowledge of traditional ways understand the great importance and symbolism of the ceremonial basket, even if they do not know the specific stories of its origin. Its beginnings—its link to the gods—provide the explanations behind the basket's design, its structure, the number of baskets needed in specific ceremonies, and its importance as a sacred space. Who wove the first basket as we know it? With few exceptions, every Navajo person asked this question, whether a medicine man or a young person learning to weave a basket for the first time, answered this question without hesitation—Changing Woman (Asdzą́ą́ Nádleehé). She is the embodiment of creation, the circular movement of time, and the perfection in creation itself. She is the mother of all Navajo people.

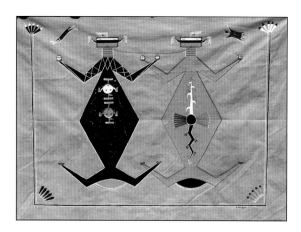

Mother Earth/Father Sky by Dennis Hathale.

Hasteen Klah, the famous medicine man who worked closely with Mary Cabot Wheelwright, told the story of when Changing Woman (Asdzáá Nádleehé) was born. Talking God went up the mountain where he found a beautiful newborn baby girl surrounded by flowers. Overjoyed, he returned to Beehoochidii (the Great God) and the other gods to give them the good news. Beehoochidii knew all about the baby and he said, "It is the child of the Earth Spirit (Mother Earth) and the Sky Spirit (Father Sky)." The gods returned to the mountain bearing gifts for the baby. First Woman brought a white shell basket and First Man, a water bowl.

From the time I was a child, my favorite sandpainting figures have been Mother Earth and Father Sky, the husband and wife embodiments of everything that surrounds us on this earth and in the heavens above. Hasteen Klah told the story of how these two spirits appeared when they were created, how their faces were painted, what they were wearing, and what they were holding. Mother Earth holds a pollen basket while Father Sky is depicted with a headdress of clouds, sometimes referred to as a cloud basket. The Museum of Indian Art and Culture in Santa Fe, New Mexico, possesses several of these cloud baskets in their collection. According to medicine man, June Blackhorse, the gods who wear this particular headdress are of the Cloud People, associated with the bringing of moisture. For example, the other name given to Father Sky, according to Hasteen Klah, is the Rain and Cloud Spirit. The Humpback yeis mentioned in the previous chapter are also of this group as well as Tó Neinilii, the Water Sprinkler and the Fringed Mouth God, Zaad doolzhaa'í.

The discussion of the origin of the basket may sometimes appear similar to the question, "What came first—the chicken or the egg?" The answer as it pertains to

Sprig of juniper next to herringbone finish.

Navajo ceremonial baskets is clear in the minds of the many Navajo people with whom I spoke. The baskets originated from the gods. The proof lies in the many references to the jewel baskets in their origin stories. When the time came for a basket to be woven as we know it today, Changing Woman is responsible for the making of that first basket. Sara Stanley, the Navajo culture teacher at Monument Valley High School in Kayenta, Arizona, talks about Changing Woman weaving the first basket. As she sat weaving under a tree, working toward the finish of the basket, she stalled, not knowing how to properly finish the basket. Talking God appeared and provided the solution to her quandary. He reached to the tree above, a juniper cedar, and plucked a sprig from the tree. The pattern from that sprig provided the inspiration for the herringbone finish, a signature of Navajo basketry today.

Carrying Baskets

Another type of basket, although not used ceremonially, deserves mention. The carrying basket, once used by the Navajo people, is still used on a limited basis by the Hopi. In my search for examples of early Navajo basketry, I was shown two examples, circa 1735, which most likely come from the Pueblita Canyon area of Dinétah, an area recognized for the earliest Navajo occupation in the Southwest. Based upon its U-shaped rod and weaving technique, one of these baskets is most likely a carrying basket similar to a basket illustrated on page 25 of George Wharton

Early Navajo carrying basket—possibly from Pueblita Canyon
area of Dinétah.
—Courtesy the U.S. Forest Service.

James' book *Indian Basketry and How to Make Indian and Other Baskets*. In the
book he mentions a legend about Monster Slayer (Naayéé' Neezghání) and the
Carrying Basket.

> In the early days of the world's history, one of their mythical heroes was
> seized by a flying monster and carried up to a dangerous ledge on a high
> mountain in New Mexico. He succeeded in killing the monster and its mate
> but was unable to get down from his perilous position. Just then he saw the
> Bat Woman (one of the mythical characters of the Navahoes) walking
> along the base of the cliff. After a good deal of persuasion, she consented
> to come up and carry him down in her basket, but she required that he
> should close his eyes before she did so. Before he closed his eyes he saw
> that the large carrying basket was held upon her back by strings as thin as
> those of a spider's web. "Grandmother," he said, "I fear to enter your bas-
> ket; the strings are too thin." "Have no fear," she replied, "I have carried a
> whole deer in this basket; the strings are strong enough to bear you." Still

Carrying basket made by Hopi artist, Darlene Lalo.

he hesitated and still she assured him. The fourth time that he expressed his fear she said: "Fill the basket with stones and you will see that I speak the truth." He did as he was bidden and she danced around with the loaded basket on her back: but the strings did not break, though they twanged like bowstrings. When he entered the basket she bade him keep his eyes shut until they reached the bottom of the cliff, as he must not see how she managed to descend. He shut his eyes and soon felt himself gradually going down; but he heard a strange flapping against the rock, which so excited his curiosity that he opened his eyes. Instantly he began to fall with dangerous rapidity, and the flapping stopped; she struck him with her stick and bade him close his eyes. Again he felt himself slowly descending, and the flapping against the rock began. Three times more he disobeyed her, and the last time they were near the bottom of the cliff, and both fell to the ground unhurt.

The story goes on to say how Bat Woman was given the feathers of the slain flying monsters. Ignoring Monster Slayer's warnings, she disobeys his instructions and all of the feathers in her basket turn into various birds who quickly escape. Thus, in this story, we now also know the origin of many species of small birds.

3. History and Archaeology of Navajo Baskets

Morning . . . Noon . . . Evening . . . Night . . . the hands of the clock spin . . . circling . . . circling in the movement of time. Art reflects life; life mirrors art. In the unfolding story of the ceremonial basket, it's deep history starts with another basket, an ancient basket, a basket by another people. That ancient basket's designs move forward into pottery. After many centuries, the designs flow back into basketry—a full cycle, yet not a complete circle, but one that starts turning . . . turning upon itself again.

Tracing and mapping the design and construction origins of historic Navajo baskets proved the greatest challenge. Where did they begin? Why are they constructed a certain way? What are the origins and meanings of the designs? Historical accounts place Navajo basket making back as far as the late 17th and early 18th centuries.

The earliest ethnohistorical record of the Navajo notes that they were making fine baskets around 1700. (Hill 1940, 400-410)

A single document, The Report of Viciente Troncoso to Fernando de la Concha, dated April 12, 1788, and describing his journey to return the Navajo headman Antonio El Pinto to his home near Big Bead Mesa, provides the only comprehensive description of Navajo culture in the latter part of the century . . . coiled baskets or "Xicaras that are called 'Navajo,'" were of exceptionally high quality. (Brugge 1980, 22)

Armed with several vague stories, my march back in time started with the finest contemporary collections and then jumped back one hundred years. This century old rich visual resource came from the Navajo basket collection of John and Jacque Foutz, long time residents of New Mexico.

John and Jacque possess a great love of Navajo ceremonial baskets and have enthusiastically collected them, particularly older ones, for nearly forty years. Although they thrill over the baskets, they, too, had no idea what the designs meant.

Hubbell Trading Post National Historic Monument in Ganado, Arizona, possesses a similarly rich collection of early Navajo basket weavings, mostly collected between 1900 and 1920. Information of their origins and meanings is lacking here as well.

A plethora of designs were being woven in the late 1800s and early 1900s. Natural curiosity forced me to wonder why, only a few decades later, the one design recognized as *the* Navajo ceremonial basket survived above all others. Armed with photographs of the Foutz collection, I started with the medicine men to get an understanding of the designs.

June Blackhorse, a respected Navajo medicine man or hataałii was very open in

Spiderwoman cross basket.
—Courtesy of John and Jacque Foutz Private Collection.

Rug with Spiderwoman crosses.
—Courtesy of Amer and Cindy Tumeh Private Collection.

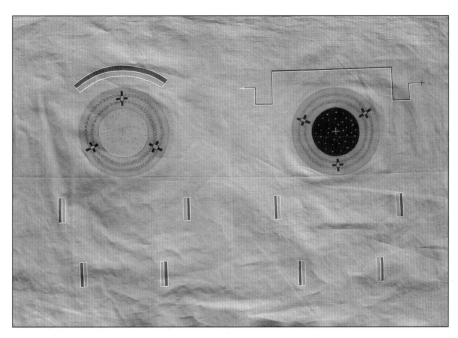

Memory painting of male and female ceremonial medicine baskets by Bruce Hathale.
—Courtesy of Georgiana Kennedy Simpson Private Collection.

his discussion of the images. As I laid down one picture after another, he discussed the design, sometimes at length, other times, merely saying, "It is just a design." The starting point was a design known as Spiderwoman or rain crosses, a pattern that is also popular on Navajo rug and blanket weavings. This particular design figured prominently in Navajo ceremonial baskets, particularly in those used for holding sacred meal during a ceremony.

> The other form of Navaho sacred basket . . . is also made of aromatic sumac, and is used in the rites to hold sacred meal. The crosses are said to represent clouds, heavy with rain, and would indicate that this basketry design may have had its origin in its use during ceremonies intended to bring the rain. (George Wharton James)

Various basket collections I viewed in the course of research for this volume contained baskets with either three or four crosses. The first basket image with this cross design shown to June contained four crosses. He was emphatic in saying that it was sometimes used as a sacred basket but that it should have three crosses, not four. Looking at the instructional aide for baskets being used for either men or women to eat from, it does indeed show a basket with only three crosses. (See Bruce Hathale memory painting of male and female baskets, above.) However, renditions

Rain cross basket with blanket
influence, early 1900s.
—Courtesy Hubbell Trading Post
National Historic Monument.

Three rain cross basket, circa late
1800s.
—Courtesy John and Jacque Foutz
Private Collection.

Rain cross baskets, circa 1900.
—Courtesy of Museum of Indian Art and Culture, Santa Fe, New Mexico.

of this meal basket in the book *Indian Basketry* by George Wharton James show a sacred meal basket with four crosses. Basket weaver Mary Holiday Black also said this particular basket should contain four crosses. While this particular basket figures prominently in ceremonies witnessed by Washington Matthews and other ethnographers in the late 1800s and early 1900s, its use has faded from existence.

Moving on to the next basket, June proclaimed, "Oh, that is the rising sun." It did indeed give the visual effect of sun rays. (See the picture of the walking sun basket, page 25.) On my first visit to the Laboratory of Anthropology in Santa Fe, New Mexico, I spoke to John Torres, a Navajo archaeologist specializing in Upper San Juan Basin archaeology and the new head curator for the Museum of Indian Art and Culture. None of the designs registered with John until I placed the "rising sun" design in front of him. He said, "Oh, the walking sun," an interesting comment after

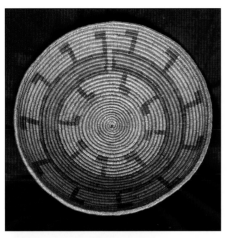

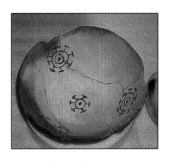

Walking sun basket.
—Courtesy of John and Jacque Foutz Private Collection.

Four walking suns pottery.—Courtesy of Museum of Indian Art and Culture, Santa Fe, NM.

Two walking suns pottery.
—Courtesy of Museum of Indian Art and Culture, Santa Fe, NM.

Oblong walking sun pottery.
—Courtesy of Museum of Indian Art and Culture, Santa Fe, NM.

June's proclamation about the same basket. "What do you mean?" I asked. "It's a common design on Anasazi pottery!" At that point I grew excited as I was beginning to discover the link and relationship of Ancestral Puebloan (Anasazi) basketry and pottery to Navajo basket design and construction. (See the pictures of the walking sun pottery above.)

In earlier studies of Navajo basketry, comparisons were made between Ancestral Puebloan and Navajo weaving techniques. They found the rod-and-bundle techniques and herringbone rim finishes to be peculiar to both groups.

> Today . . . the Navajo represent the only Southwestern group to manufacture two-rod and bundle coiled basketry. (Weltfish 1930)

> There seems to be little room for doubt that the Navajo took over this trait from the earlier inhabitants of the Pueblo plateau after they arrived in approximately their present position. (Tschopik 1939, 127)

> Rims are always woven in a herringbone pattern . . . clearly another element of the coiling complex that the Navajos acquired from the Anasazi, this

Herringbone rim finish of Ancestral Puebloan basket on the left (Courtesy of Edge of the Cedars Museum, Blanding, Utah.) and a contemporary Navajo basket on the right.

technique was common as early as Basketmaker II times (200 BC to AD 400) and continued in use through Pueblo III (AD 100 to 1400). (Kidder and Guernsey 1919, 30; Morris and Burgh 1941, 23)

Because it [herringbone rim finish] was used on old Navajo baskets but not on the old baskets of the Southern Paiutes, it appears to have been adopted by the Paiutes when they began making wedding baskets for the Navajos . . . (McGreevy 1985, 31, Whiteford 1988, 36-38)

By the end of the 1800s, the two-rod-and-bundle coiled basket was on the wane and was being replaced by three-rod coil foundations. This coiling technique may have been assimilated by Navajo weavers at the same time they learned to make the two-rod-and-bundle baskets. It is noted that the Eastern Pueblo people were using both techniques as late as Pueblo IV times (AD 1400-1800). (Morris and Burgh 1941, 23) Did the Navajo weavers learn the technique from them or did they pick it up from the nearby Pai and Western Apache tribes, both practitioners of the three-rod technique?

What becomes more interesting in this spiral back in time is looking even earlier toward the source of the first Puebloan pottery design. The answer? Baskets! Beautiful baskets preceded the pottery-making periods, and in studies and comparisons

Ancestral Puebloan basket with a design that later translated into pottery design. —American Museum of Natural History.

Ancestral Puebloan pottery design directly influenced by previous Basketmaker period basket designs. —Museum of Indian Art & Culture.

Ancestral Puebloan basket with a design that later translated into pottery and much later into Navajo baskets.—American Museum of Natural History.

Late 1800s Navajo basket. —Courtesy Foutz Collection.

Navajo basket design similar to pottery design found in Anasazi pot retrieved from Grave 153, Site 6 Navajo Reservation. Basket from Foutz Private Collection. Pot from Gregory/Hellman Anthropological Papers.

of Basketmaker period weavings and the pottery that followed in the Puebloan periods, it seems that the overwhelming design influence originated with baskets.

> The first pottery was crude, limited in range of form, and sparsely decorat-
> ed with designs for the most part taken over from basketry . . . Gregory and
> Hellman 1926, 198)

What brought the Navajo people to this part of the country in the first place? In
an interesting discussion with John Torres of the Museum of Indian Art and Culture,
he mentioned obsidian, an important weapon-making material. Moving south from
the Yellowstone area, the next location where extensive quantities of obsidian existed was near the area occupied by the Jemez people of New Mexico. In Andrew
Hunter Whiteford's book, *Southwestern Indian Baskets: Their History and Their*

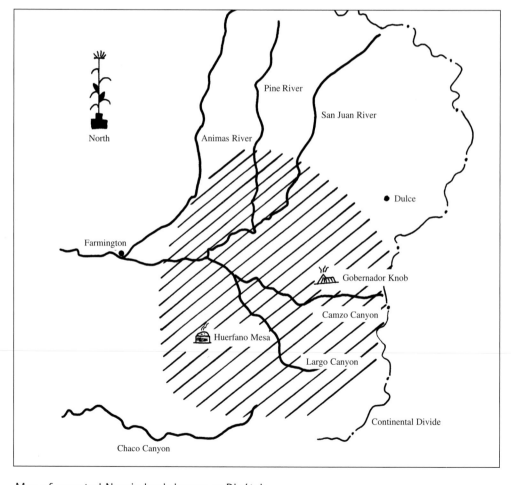

Map of ancestral Navajo lands known as Dinétah.
—Courtesy Jim Copeland, Archaeologist, Bureau of Land Management.

Makers, Whiteford refers to the most extensive contact period between the Navajo and Pueblo people occurring between 1700 and 1770. This follows one school of archaeological thought, which credits the Pueblo Revolt of 1680 and subsequent Spanish reconquest of 1692 as the watershed event resulting in substantial Pueblo influence on Navajo culture. Current Southwestern archaeological debate rages over the impact of the Pueblo Revolt, the subsequent exodus of Pueblo people into Dinétah, and the extent of their influence on and integration with the Navajo people. Jim Copeland, archaeologist for the Bureau of Land Management, along with numerous other scholars, follow a different school of thought, which holds that there is enough evidence in the archaeological record to show a much earlier interaction between the Navajo and Pueblo people. For example, some Navajo rock art elements show imagery that clearly show Pueblo influence, yet, were produced prior to the European contact era, which began approximately 1540. Gobernador Polychrome, a Navajo type of pottery most prominent in the 1700s, has been found at sites dated prior to the Pueblo Revolt. Finally, it has more recently been established that this contact occurred much earlier with the traded chert of Jemez origin appearing in Navajo archaeological sites dated approximately 1400. John Torres figures the earliest Navajo contact with Pueblo people occurred with the Jemez Pueblo people who were in the furthest outlying village and who were nearest the chert. For example, in one upper San Juan Basin Navajo site dated 1541, thirty thousand lithic artifacts derived from this particular chert were found. The importance of the obsidian should not be underestimated, as emphasized in this reference found in the *Memorial of Fray Alonso de Benavides*:

> There is flint in their mountains, he says, and the Christian Indians [Pueblo Indians] greatly desire it. They make expeditions to get the stone, but the

Similarities were evident in the look and treatment of early Navajo rock art and early Jemez topknot design pottery.

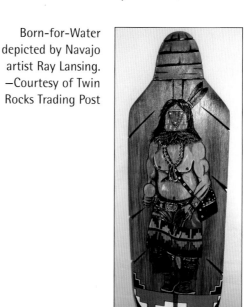

Born-for-Water
depicted by Navajo
artist Ray Lansing.
—Courtesy of Twin
Rocks Trading Post

Late 1800s topknot design basket as seen
in Andrew Hunter Whiteford's book.
—Courtesy the School of American
Research, Indian Arts Research Center,
Santa Fe, New Mexico.

Navajos, two or three thousand strong, come out to fight them, and there is
much killing.

John took me down into the museum's collection where we looked at early
Jemez pottery. What we found provided another eye opening experience. The hair
bundle design (tsiiyééł), which appears on the mask of Born-for-Water, one of the

This Navajo rock
image in Dinétah is of
Jóhonaa'éí, bearer of
the sun, and father of
the Hero Twins. The
image features the
topknot design.
—Courtesy Jim
Copeland,
Archaeologist, Bureau
of Land Management.

Navajo rock art of War Gods features a hair bundle design from Dinétah.
—Courtesy Jim Copeland, Archaeologist, Bureau of Land Management.

Navajo Hero Twins and his father, Jóhonaa'éí, is evident in early Jemez pottery. (See the topknot design pottery, page 29.) Another archaeologist, Jim Copeland, of the Bureau of Land Management, acknowledges that the hair bundle design figures prominently in early Navajo rock art, but he does not feel comfortable in making the leap between Jemez pottery design and the later emergence of the topknot design on Navajo masks, baskets, and rock art.

Interestingly, the Jemez people today have a special relationship with the Navajo. My friend, Felicia Loretto, recalls a feast day held every year at Jemez Pueblo on November 12th that honors their Navajo friends. The early writings of the Franciscan Fathers make note of this special relationship as well.

> While the Navaho are permitted to attend some of the ceremonies of the neighboring Pueblo, this is particularly true in regard to the Jemez tribe, whose shamans at times are invited to hold ceremonies over Navaho patients. (Franciscan Fathers 1910, 394)

Spirited discussion continues regarding early Navajo and Pueblo contact. In addition to the Jemez people, Navajo interaction with the Zia, San Ildefonso, Santa Clara, Acoma, Zuni, and Hopi tribes is well documented. The difficulty for Southwestern scholars lies not so much in the lack of an archaeological record, but as Jim Copeland aptly identifies the question as, "What is [the archaeological material's proper] context?"

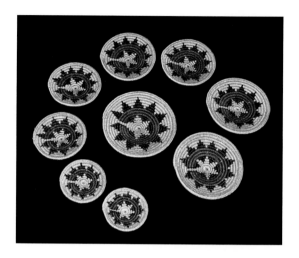

Unusual Navajo ceremonial set.
—Courtesy of Simpson Family Collection.

Only a few decades into the Twentieth Century, the variety of Navajo basket designs inexplicably faded until only one design remained in the form of the ceremonial basket we know today. By viewing hundreds of baskets woven during this period (the late 1800s into the early 1900s), I noticed a rich diversity of Navajo basketry designs. Other earlier researchers have made similar observations.

Several different designs are found on Navajo ceremonial baskets dating from the nineteenth century (for a thorough account, see Whiteford 1988, 36-37, figs. 26, 27, 28). The Navajo originally manufactured a

Contemporary ceremonial basket woven by Mary Black.
—Courtesy of Simpson Family Collection.

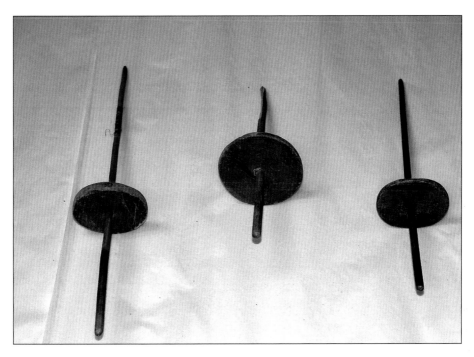

Weaving spindles, probably from Pueblita Canyon Navajo archaeological site, circa 1735.
—Courtesy U.S. Forest Service.

variety of different styles of baskets for utilitarian and ritual uses (Franciscan Fathers 1910, 293-294).

Although most styles and designs became obsolete during the late nineteenth or early twentieth century as new forms of containers such as metal pots, buckets, cups, and plates were acquired through trade, (Whiteford 1988:32) baskets continue to be made on a limited basis for use in ceremonies. The distinctive design . . . (See the Navajo ceremonial set on page 32.) has been made continually until the present and is the most pervasive of all designs found on Navajo baskets today. Baskets with this design are commonly referred to as "Navajo wedding baskets." This is a misnomer, for although they are an important element in wedding ceremonies, their ritual and nonritual contexts are much broader. Baskets are inverted and used as drums in several ceremonies. They are used as portions of certain masks in the nine-night ceremonies. (Tschopik 1940, 447) As noted by Irene Kee, baskets serve as containers for the yucca suds used in ceremonial baths, as well as for religious paraphernalia, sacred cornmeal, and medicinal herbs. In addition, they are frequently used on a day-to-day basis as storage containers for jewelry. (Wesley Thomas, interview by the Mauren Trudelle Schwarz, November 12, 1994)

Navajo basket possibly from Pueblita Canyon area of Dinétah, circa 1735. —Courtesy U.S. Forest Service

At this time it is somewhat difficult to determine how and when Ancestral Puebloan basketry and pottery designs found their way into Navajo basketry. Few examples of Navajo basketry made prior to the nineteenth century exist. Three groups of baskets were viewed. The first set belongs to the U.S. Forest Service office in Bloomfield, New Mexico. Unfortunately, this group was brought in by a private individual, so the provenance cannot be absolutely confirmed. Several aspects of this particular collection, however, bring Rachel Miller, the Forest Service archaeologist stationed at Bloomfield, and Jim Copeland, a Bureau of Land Management archaeologist and noted early Navajo scholar, to the conclusion that this collection is of early Navajo origin. They believe the items most likely originated in Pueblita Canyon, a location containing well-documented early Navajo sites. The two baskets were brought in with other identifiable Navajo artifacts, including several weaving spindles and gourd cups. The remnant of the other basket is very similar to carrying baskets historically used by the Navajo people and currently being used by the Hopi on a limited basis. I asked Rachel if there was any possibility of the group being Ancestral Puebloan (Anasazi) in origin. She said, "No, the dating is all wrong. These items were made post Anasazi occupation." (See examples of Pueblita Navajo basket on page 34, Pueblita Navajo carrying basket on page 18, and Pueblita spindles on page 33.)

The second and most spectacular group of baskets reside in the Museum of Indian Art and Culture collection in Santa Fe, New Mexico. This set consists of several crown headdress baskets (further detailed in the chapter Sacred Space, beginning on page 61.) included in a larger collection known as the Palluche Cache. The site is located in Palluche Canyon and is dated in the Refugee Period, which spans 1698-1775. These baskets represent the most stunning example, of not only early Navajo ceremonial basketry but the direct relationship between Navajo and Ancestral Puebloan weaving techniques. Ceremonial baskets used in this manner are typically painted inside and out, so the design elements are somewhat difficult to discern, although one of the baskets clearly shows a design that looks similar to those found on Ancestral Puebloan baskets. The small, tight coils typical of Ancestral Puebloan basketry, as well as many Navajo baskets woven in the late 1800s, however, is clearly evident in this set of baskets.

Fannie King with her basket inspired by a pottery shard design.

Finally, a pitch basket (tóshjeeh) in the Navajo Nation Museum collection was found at Shaft House Ruin, a Pueblita site located in the Largo Canyon area of Dinétah. This defensive site dates between 1712 and 1750. This particular basket is perhaps the most touching. It was found containing numerous small weaving tools, including several spindles and battens. The spindles are smaller than contemporary versions, which leads us to speculate whether that is due to the people being smaller, or perhaps this basket contains tools once utilized by a child. This basket is a stunning precursor to today's pitch baskets.

Part of the challenge in tracing the first appearance of Ancestral Puebloan design elements in Navajo basketry lies in a question we must ask ourselves, "Where did Navajo people first see these designs?" Based on the discussion set forth above, the most likely scenario is that the Navajo acquired basket designs and weaving techniques directly from their Puebloan neighbors. In addition, Ancestral Puebloan pottery, whether whole pieces or shards, are as much a part of the Navajo landscape as the red rock mesas. Although a traditional taboo exists that a Navajo person must avoid contact with Ancestral Puebloan ruins and artifacts, many Navajo people live on land littered with the detritus of the previous Ancestral Puebloan occupation. Just as these designs continue to influence many artists today, it is now known

Hubbell basket collection on the ceiling of Hubbell Trading Post. Most Navajo baskets in this collection were acquired between 1900 and 1920.

Catalogue and Price List

Navajo Blankets
& Indian Curios

J. L. HUBBELL
I N D I A N   T R A D E R

Ganado, Apache County, *Arizona*
Branch Store: Keam's Cañon, Arizona

Plain white ceremonial blanket.
5¼ x 6........................$8.00 to $10.00

Women's girdles, woven of fine spun scarlet wool with designs embossed with thread in black, white and green, from 3½ to 6 inches wide and from 8 to 10 feet long ....$3.00 to $3 50

Antelope dance sash, white cotton, decorative fringes, 8 in. wide...........   ...$5.00

Squaw shawl.
3¼ x 4......$7 50 to $10.00

Basketry

Moqui shallow discoid plaques, displaying elaborately plaited designs.

10 inch..$0.50	14 inch..$1.50
11 inch.. .75	17 inch.. 1.75
12 inch. .1.00	18 inch.. 2.00
20 inch........$2.50	

Oraibi plaques of **dyed yucca** fibre, wrapped in coils.

10 in...$0.50	16 in...$1.25
12 in... .75	18 in... 1.50
14 in... 1.00	19 in... 1.57
20 in.... ....$2.00	

Navajo marriage baskets, about 15 inches in diameter.
.... $4.00 to $7.50

Navajo wicker water bottles.....
.... $2.00 to $5.00

8

J.L. Hubbell Catalog featuring, among other things, Navajo "marriage" baskets and "Moqui" (Ancestral Puebloan) pottery, circa 1910.—Courtesy Hubbell Trading Post National Historical Site.

that this was yet another avenue for design influence in Navajo basketry. This theory was demonstrated recently when Fannie King, a weaver from Navajo Mountain, brought her latest weaving into the Twin Rocks Trading Post. Fannie is Navajo and her husband is Paiute. My husband, Steve, commented that her latest design looked Anasazi (Ancestral Puebloan). Fannie stated, "Oh yes . . . I had picked up a pottery shard and liked the design, so I wove it into the basket."

Another possible and more recent realm of influence may have come from some of the early traders. Lorenzo Hubbell had a great love of basketry and also sold quantities of Ancestral Puebloan pottery. (See the picture of the Hubbell basket collection on the ceiling, page 36.) It is quite possible that weavers frequenting the trading post might have seen some of the pottery and incorporated the designs into their baskets. This type of influence from an outsider is certainly true, for example, in the recent evolution of Paiute weaving design. Paiute weavers were exposed to images of baskets from the Fred Harvey collection, a group of weavings including examples of Navajo baskets woven in the late 1800s. The bottom line is that there is no question that Ancestral Puebloan basket designs had an impact on a number of weavers creating baskets around the 1800s and early 1900s. Examples of several of these basket designs are found in the American Museum of Natural History Collection. Because of the dearth of Navajo basket artifacts predating this time period, the question of pinpointing the start of Ancestral Puebloan design influence in Navajo basketry remains an open issue.

By the end of the 1800s significant economic and political shifts were occurring on the Navajo reservation, which appear to have impacted the overall production of Navajo basketry. Several anthropologists note that basket weaving taboos became so restrictive that they virtually quelled Navajo basket production. As the Navajo population increased during this same period, it became necessary for them to turn to their neighbors, the Paiutes and Utes, to fill the increasing demand for ceremonial baskets. The vast contribution that Paiute and Ute weavers made to the continuing production of ceremonial baskets cannot be ignored. Ethnographer Susan Brown

Eastern Sierra Paiute burden basket, winnowing tray, and seed beater, circa 1900.
—Courtesy of Georgiana Kennedy Simpson Private Collection.

Unusual ceremonial basket set woven by Paiute weaver Rose Ann Whiskers.
The baskets measure from 2¾" to 5" in diameter.
—Courtesy Georgiana Kennedy Simpson Private Collection.

McGreevy documented this phenomenon in her book *Translating Tradition: Basketry Arts of the San Juan Paiute.* The Paiute's relationship with the Navajo was a double-edged sword. While they were being raided by the Navajo, a trade relationship was established whereby the San Juan Paiutes were producing pitch basket water jugs for trade with the Navajos. Pamela Bunte suggests that this represented the beginning of basketry trade for the San Juan Paiutes in what was to develop as an important source of revenue for the Paiute people. (Bunte, 1985, 11) Both superintendent Janus of the Western Navajo Agency (1909) and the Franciscan Fathers (1910) made note of an active trade of water bottles and ceremonial baskets. By the 1930s, in some areas of the Navajo Reservation, it is believed that the Paiute weavers were the sole suppliers of ceremonial baskets to the Navajo people. (Stewart, 1938; Billy 1983, 322; Morez 1982, 139-140) Paiute weavers differentiated between their twined pitch baskets, burden baskets, winnowing trays, and seed beaters, what they refer to as "old-timer baskets" that preserve Paiute tradition and the "wedding baskets" that produce revenue. (McGreevy, 1985, 26) (See the picture of traditional Paiute baskets, page 38.)

> Because the Navajo wedding basket continues to provide a reliable source of income, it is the type most frequently made by San Juan Paiute weavers even today. In 1974, Sandra Corrie Newman wrote, "My basket teacher, a Paiute [this was Marie Lehi] said her great-grandmother learned to weave the [wedding] basket from Navajo women. Paiute women, mainly on the western edge of the [Navajo] reservation . . . continue to supply the basket for Navajo use." According to Newman, wedding baskets were the principal type made by Lehi and her family at the time of her research in the early 1970s. (1985:personal communication.) More recently, Bunte has observed numerous Navajo visits to Paiute camps to obtain wedding baskets (1984). (McGreevy, 1985, 27)

Interestingly, and somewhat inadvertently, contemporary Paiute baskets have become a repository for some of the old Navajo basket designs. Paiute weavers were shown baskets from the Fred Harvey Collection, a group of baskets possessing a variety of designs being woven in the late 1800s. While the vast majority of these designs faded from Navajo basket making, they continue to thrive among Paiute weavers. Also, there are several Paiute weavers whose basket construction more closely resembles the weaving technique of late 1800s baskets as well as Ancestral Puebloan weavings.

Today, unless a ceremonial basket from the turn of the twentieth century is specifically documented as Navajo, it is difficult, if not impossible, to determine if the basket is of Navajo, Paiute, or Ute origin. Navajo culture interpreter, Geno Bahe, of the Hubbell Trading Post National Historic Site, believes the subsequent decline in the variety of basket designs resulted from the decrease in Navajo weavers and the increase of Ute and Paiute basket makers who specifically focused on producing the ceremonial basket design. I also imagine there may have been a traditional backlash against many new and abundant designs, especially those related to Anasazi pottery designs. This is best explained by medicine men John Holiday and June Blackhorse. When they were shown the many designs being made in the late 1800s, they were willing to address the designs, but both were pointed in their statements saying that all of these other designs had no business being made—there is only one true ceremonial

Navajo ceremonial set woven by Ute weaver Susan Whyte (1934-1994).
—Courtesy Simpson Family Collection

basket design and it is the one required for ceremonies today. A century after the expansion of designs in the late 1800s, a similar trend is occurring in Navajo basket weaving with a richness and variety never before witnessed in any form of Native American basketry. Both medicine men feel strongly that all of these other designs should not be executed. June Blackhorse put it this way: "A long time ago, we did not record any of the [sandpainting] designs. Today, many of these designs are done, but just for money, and they do not know why they are doing those designs. I feel what they are doing will finally destroy them. The designs need to be drawn back into the ceremonial basket."

The basket is a representation of this earth. The start is the emergence place. The white in the middle is the earth. The first black designs are the mountains. The red is the rainbow. The outside black designs are clouds and the outside white design represents the waters of the world.

Molly Yellowman as told to her by her mother, Gladys Yellowman

An exaggerated emergence opening
in a ceremonial basket woven by Bonnie Bitsinnie.
—Courtesy Simpson Family Collection.

4. Baskets as a Reflection of the Landscape

One of the early, somewhat vague, stories I heard about the wedding basket design mentioned mountains, clouds, and a rainbow (nááts'íílid). For many years, we gave out this information in the trading post until finally realizing that we really did not know the full story behind the basket design, how the pattern evolved, and why it is so important today. The journey to discovery led my children and me on what I called "Chasing Rainbows" adventures—trips in search of rainbows to photograph. Rainbow hunting in the southwestern sky generously rewards the alert seeker. I'm not sure what is more spectacular—spotting a triple rainbow or witnessing a complete arc. One of my favorite stories is told by my friend, Jenelia Benally. She talked about what I call "sun dogs," which are rainbow spots in the sky. When you see two of them along the horizon, they are said to be the sun's jacla (jaatł'óół) earrings. I like that imagery.

Our first "Chasing Rainbows" adventure took place on and below a mesa in the Monument Valley area. Allison Billy, my kids, and I were photographing Etta Rock demonstrating the application of pitch to a traditional basket jug. While waiting for Etta to emerge from her house, I gazed out in all directions. The land gently sloped downward through sagebrush giving the impression that if you curled yourself in a ball, you could roll right down into the heart of Monument Valley. Looking west, the

Four Directions set woven by Peggy Black.
—Courtesy Simpson Family Collection.

rounded, lonely dome of Navajo Mountain receded into the purple haze of distance. Looking north, the snow-capped peak of Blue Mountain commanded the skyline with the double buttes of the Bear's Ears off to the left. The clouds shifted and danced throughout the afternoon. I closed my eyes and imagined the light moving through the cycle of the day, following the pattern of the four directional colors: white for the dawn light, blue for the day, yellow for the evening, and black for the night. The promise of changing weather drifted in with the winds, the clouds further shifting the light and teasing us with the promise of moisture. We waited and watched to see if the sunset would cast its glow through a rain shower and honor us with a burst of rainbow color. I experienced my first of many "Aha!" moments in this project. As a Navajo person striving to live in the traditional, balanced way, how can one not be moved to express the surrounding landscape and elements that so firmly provide bearings and anchors for your place in the world?

John Holiday learned his medicine ways seventy-three years ago. In introducing his credentials, he carried us back through eight generations of medicine men. In other words, he was conveying that his knowledge is very old and is borne on the shoulders of many wise men. In my research, it was mentioned that men who possess knowledge of medicine ways taught prior to the Long Walk period were considered to be the best reservoirs of traditional knowledge. John certainly fits into this category. When he sat down with the basket, he took us through a wholly different interpretation of the imagery conveyed by the designs.

> The center of the basket rests on a weaving spindle, the type used for spinning wool in preparation for weaving rugs. The basket represents the earth and the movement of the earth is controlled by five coyotes; a white one, a turquoise one, a yellow one, a black one, and a darker black one, working together to spin the world and create the passage of the day and movement through time as we know it. The red design represents the red sand on which we walk in Dinétah. The outer black designs represent the clouds. (John Holiday, interviewed by the author, April 16, 2001)

Their land, Dinétah, the People's Land, is represented every time a ceremonial basket is made. Medicine man, June Blackhorse, provides this eloquent description of the landscape in the basket:

> Now, I'm going to talk about nahagha' (ceremony). I'm going to talk about the basket and how it is used in ceremony. The center of the basket is where the water exists. After the water are the plants. The inside black design represents the mountains. The red band is the rainbow. The black on the outside of the rainbow are the clouds. Finally, the sunlight is the white area beyond the clouds. The reason the basket looks like everything is bursting out from the center is that it represents everything growing out from the basket.

Double Ceremonial woven by Kee Bitsinnie, circa 1985.
—Courtesy Simpson Family Collection.

It was in this way that June Blackhorse was taught when he started his medicine ways instruction in 1965. This concept of the Navajo universe being represented by a circle was noted by Louise Lamphere (1969, 286-288) in an article titled "Hogans, Sacred Circles and Symbols—The Navajo Use of Space" by Susan Kent of the University of New Mexico.

> The Navajo think of their cosmos as a circle where the "sky horizon edge" . . . meets the "earth horizon edge" . . . The circular horizon is divided into "light phenomena." Each has an "inner form" . . . which is male or female, and each is associated with one of 4 directions and one of 4 colors.

> The order in which directions are named (east, south, west, and north) follows the clockwise motion of the sun as it advances across the sky when the observer is oriented to the south. In sum, the circular horizon, the 2 sexes, the 4 directions, the 4 colors, and the clockwise movement of the sun are the Navajo distinctions basic to the cosmological scheme.

In a later conversation, June talked about how none of the things we see in our surroundings could exist if the basket did not exist. He spoke specifically about the sunlight area of the basket, the white area between the black cloud design and the rim of the basket. This area represents all of the light experienced throughout the day: white dawn light, blue midday light, yellow afternoon light, and the black of night. Each type of light provides special nourishment to all living things, for example, plants with white flowers are nourished by the early dawn light, while other plants with yellow flowers are nourished by the rays of the late afternoon sun. The Holy People are said to reside where the light of dawn exists at the place where the sun's rays first shoot upward at the beginning of each day. It is a place where everything is silent and holy. It is for this reason that Navajo people must rise early in the morning, turn toward the dawn light, and ask for special blessings from the Holy People. In the traditional way, a person rises early and runs toward that light, gathering the strength, blessings, and good health it provides.

The blue sun rays are said to emanate from the south. These rays nourish the four sacred plants of the Navajo people: squash, corn, tobacco, and beans. It is the time of great activity during each day. As the day proceeds into the late afternoon, the yellow rays of the west take over. After working all day, it is a time to relax, to slow down. As my interpreter, Molly Yellowman, phrased it, "You know what it is like when you look at the color yellow. It calms you down." Finally, the black light of the north, the darkness, is the time for all living things to rest. June spoke about how each of us reflects these colors in the way we dress. For example, a nurse or doctor in white is asking for the blessings of the early dawn light. June tends to wear a balance of colors so that he may receive the sunlight blessings from all directions. He stated that most people don't intentionally pick their clothing colors each day, but rather unconsciously pick colors depending on where strength is needed for that particular day. Looking down at my black jacket and pants, I decided I was definitely invoking the color of night due to the sleep deprivation experienced during this writing project.

Different accounts of the symbolism of the basket abound, especially as it relates to the surrounding landscape. One of the earliest accounts was provided by the anthropologist, Stanley Fishler. In 1950, he was gathering information from a Navajo religious practitioner named Frank Goldtooth who provided the following account:

> The center spot in the basket represents the beginning of this earth as the Navajo emerged from the cane. The white portion surrounding the center spot is the earth. The black represents the six or ten sacred mountains to the Navajo and forms a boundary-line of the early Navajo people. . . . Only six mountains are represented in some of the baskets, for that is the number of mountains brought up from below during the flood. . . . Above the represented earth are clouds which have many colors represented within them, as do real clouds above the earth. . . . The white and black clouds are important. They represent the same thing—the making of rain. The rain represented in the basket is to bring comfort to the earth—to make plants and all things grow. . . . Next to the mountains is a red or brown section which represents the sun-rays. It also means the rainbow spectrum upon which the gods travel. The sun-ray is to make things on earth grow and to make things go the right way. This sun-ray in the basket is to bring comfort to the earth, to make plants and all things grow and to keep the earth and the people warm. The number of the clouds has no significance. The finish point of the basket always goes to the east. (Goldtooth, quoted in Fishler 1954, 208-209)

To understand the design reflected in every ceremonial basket, it is important to step back and more fully detail Navajo philosophy. In Gladys A. Reichard's book, *Navajo Medicine Man Sandpaintings*, she beautifully explains this starting point that guides the balance in a basket—a person's life, and all their surroundings.

The Navajo religion must be considered as a design in harmony, a striving for rapport between man and every phase of nature, the earth and the waters under the earth, the sky and the "land beyond the sky" and of course, the earth and everything on and in it. In order to establish and continue this rapport the beings which dwell in all these places must be controlled. All of this rules out the idea of a single god, Great Spirit, God, monotheism, or whatever one may prefer to call it. In order to understand the Navajo viewpoint we have to reconstruct our ideas of religion and allow them to embrace things we have not before included, but at the same time we may not allow ourselves the comfort of categories or catch-words such as magic, animism, nature worship and the like, for the Navajo religion is so inclusive that it touches upon all of these, and what is more, in it each one of these overlaps the others.

One of the fundamental premises is the belief that nothing in the universe is for naught, but that the smallest entity has its purpose in helping man. Since man is only one of the infinite number of things in nature, he is no more important than anything else, a seed of corn, for instance, or a fly. But, in order to make his life on the earth tolerable, man must have control of that seed or fly.

By weaving a basket well, the artist is putting all of the world into balance. It is as if to say, "All is well. See how our beginning place, the plants, the waters, the mountains, the clouds in the sky, everything is as it should be. Look at this basket. Use this basket, knowing that everything is in balance; everything is where it belongs."

The Kin łichíi'nii Basket.

Interlude

The designs on the basket are a visual record of Navajo history from the emergence through every phase of life in this world. They record the critical events in the construction of every aspect of the Navajo universe and in Navajo history. As a visual record of the "natural order" of the Navajo cosmos, the designs on baskets serve as mnemonic devices by which life can be ordered.

—Maureen Trudelle Schwarz 1997, 39

The Story of the Kin łichíi'nii Basket

I came into this family at grandmother's wedding. I was the special basket for the ceremony, the one in which the sacred mush is mixed and blessed by the man leading the ceremony. Grandmother, Shimá sání, and grandfather, Shicheii, came together at this wedding. The sacred corn mush was placed in me and blessed with the corn meal. Starting from east to west, a line of cornmeal was drawn across the mush, then from south to north. Then a circle of cornmeal went around my edges. This cornmeal helped bless and strengthen the mush I was protecting. The mush I contained was sacred and meant to help the new couple in their life together.

I have been in this family for a long time. My family is Kin łichíi'nii, the Red House clan. As you can see, I am much older now and faded from the many years of use. I am now in the special care of one of the granddaughters. I was almost lost a few years ago when one of the family members no longer believed in the Navajo way and wanted to get rid of me, but fortunately, I was rescued in time. Anytime the family has a special ceremony, I am brought out for that ceremony whether it be a wedding; a Kinaaldá, a girl's coming of age celebration; or for blessings of the family's jewelry during other ceremonies. When I am not at a ceremony, the family jewelry and special medicine items are kept in me to protect them and bring blessings and good fortune to the family.

The Story of the Kin łichíi'nii Basket
as told to the author on July 26, 2001

5. Symbol of Life

It is a representation of your life. The beginning is like the whorl at the top of a baby's head. The beginning white portion is how you are as you are starting to grow. The first black designs represent your brothers and sisters. The red is a representation of you getting married. The black above that are your children and if there is red above that, your grandchildren. As it goes back to the white, it represents how you are growing old and how you are reaching full circle in your life.

Betty Yazzie, 3/1/01

Many families possess a basket like the Kin łichíi'nii basket, one that serves as a reminder of who they are as a people, the Diné and Dinétah, the Navajo homeland. Allison Billy explains, "The basket represents your mind and when the basket being is held by a family, it holds the minds of your family. If the basket is turned or spun, it is like you are twisting your mind and your family's mind." The basket speaks on many levels by showing the path toward a balanced and productive life. Geno Bahe, interpreter of Navajo culture for Hubbell Trading Post National Historic Site, was taught by his great-grandfather about the basket as it relates to each Navajo person's life. He further expands on the thoughts introduced by Betty Yazzie.

Betty Yazzie, a former Navajo culture instructor at the Rough Rock Demonstration School. She is currently a senior citizens coordinator.

When a baby is born, that baby is connected to and nourished by its mother via the umbilical cord. After birth, the umbilical cord is buried near the home to remind each person from where they came. When one Navajo person wishes to know where another Navajo person is from, they ask, "Where is your umbilical cord buried?" In this way, they may truly ascertain from where a person originates. The center, the start, of the basket represents the umbilical. A baby's life journey begins with its family. The mother and her sisters help nourish the baby. At the place where the black design begins, this is the representation of where the child starts to speak. The white gaps between the black design symbolize the parents stepping in again to help the child. As more and more of the black design appears, what it is saying is that you are gaining the knowledge you are supposed to know for living this life.

Every parent of teenage children will relate to this next thought. At the place where the design becomes completely black, it is where you believe you know everything. No wonder teenagers argue so much with their parents! All of the knowledge that has been gained to this point is sealed by the rainbow. Geno explained the remainder of the basket's design:

The rainbow (nááts'íílid) provides protection for every bit of knowledge you wish to keep for yourself at this point whether it be physical, in your mind, or in your soul. The rainbow is like a covering or a seal protecting all of this knowledge. As you move out of the rainbow back into more black design, you are now moving into the teaching phase of your life. All of the knowledge you gained previously must now be shared with others. The alternating colors of black and white in these coils is like the progression of grey hair on your head. You are getting older and wiser, but as the white gaps become wider, you are also starting to forget. When you move into the area on the outer coils of the basket, the design becomes all white again. You are elderly and in effect, going back into a "baby" stage. The Navajo people do not mourn the passing of an elderly person because they have lived a complete life. The braid rim is like another seal. If you notice on a ceremonial basket, the ending of the rim is aligned with the beginning of the basket as if to say,

Geno Bahe in front of the Hubbell Trading Post.

"Life ends back where it began." All of your knowledge goes back to the beginning. Navajo people do not believe in an after-life, but rather that all of the challenges you went through, all of the knowledge you gained and shared makes it easier for the younger people following behind you.

The basket comes into play immediately in a person's life, even before birth in ceremonies performed for the pregnant mother. Navajo medicine man, June Blackhorse, talks about the introduction of the basket into a person's life.

> In the old ways, a Hózhǫǫjí (The Beauty Way) was performed when a baby was born or when the baby comes home and the basket is there. Each ring of the basket is like ten years in a person's life. It is like little kids are standing in the basket as their place to grow. That is why you don't turn a basket over their heads because that will cause them to stop growing. That is the way of life in the basket. For the rest of your life, you will use the basket. There should be twelve coils in the basket to symbolize one living a long and productive life.

John Holiday echoes this thought in his explanation of the representation of growth from the basket. He said, "A person is like corn and it grows from there (he points to the center of the basket). From there, you grow and blossom (his fingers spiral outward from the center). It is not that your life ends at the ending point of the basket, but rather when you die, everything goes back to the beginning (his finger moves from the last stitch of the rim, down the spirit break, and back to the center)."

The basket comes out again at the First Laugh Party, a celebration of the baby's vitality and the time of giving the baby its Navajo name. It is believed that if the baby survives to this time, he is more likely to move forward in his life and that first laugh represents his first genuine expression of personhood. This celebration was given for my son, Grange. Whoever makes the baby laugh first must sponsor a celebration for the baby. Priscilla Sagg and her sister, Molly Yellowman, put together the party, fixing one of our local favorites, Navajo tacos. We used the wedding basket my husband, Steve, gave me when we were married. Another helper, Sharlene Redhorse, acquired the important rock salt. After the food was prepared, Priscilla placed Grange on her lap. Each person filed by with their plate of food to receive the gift of the rock salt from Grange. This celebration assured that Grange will be generous in his life.

The next appearance of the basket is during the Kinaaldá, a girl's coming of age ceremony. Preferably, two baskets will be used during this ceremony. One basket is used for carrying and protecting the sacred cornmeal and for ceremonial baths. The

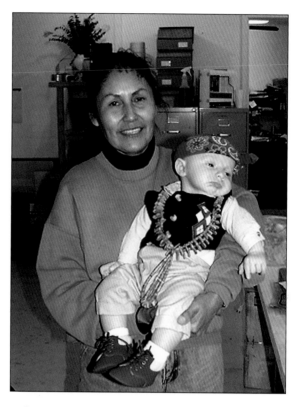

Priscilla Sagg, the provider of Grange's first laugh.

other basket holds personal belongings like the family jewelry, the initiate's personal corn pollen, and other medicine items. The girl keeps this basket beside her during the ceremony. People attending the Kinaaldá may bring other baskets holding their own belongings. They put a blanket in front of the initiate and the medicine man places the baskets in front of them to be blessed. Other items such as saddles, saddle blankets, weaving tools, college books, book bags, and any other items for which one wishes a special blessing can be blessed at this time. Geno Bahe explains that this blessing will guarantee abundance. It is as if to say, for example, that your jewelry will not only be protected, but will multiply.

The symbology of the basket is important during the Kinaaldá as Changing Woman, the weaver of the first basket, is the embodiment of the ideal woman in Navajo culture. The young woman strives to be like Changing Woman. As part of her responsibilities during the ceremony, the initiate takes cornmeal that has been piled into a mound on a blanket and carries it in the basket where it is mixed into the cake. When the cake is poured down into the earth, she carries cornmeal in the basket over to the place where the cake is being put into the earth. The girl stands toward the sun and carries the basket with cornmeal on her left side. With her right hand, she sprinkles cornmeal from east to west, then south to north, and finally clockwise around the cake being careful to leave an opening in the east. Then, anyone else who wishes for something can get cornmeal while the girl is holding the basket and make an offering to the cake.

Navajo medicine man, June Blackhorse, states that a woman should have a second Kinaaldá ceremony. The first ceremony assures the birth and health of male babies. The second ceremony guarantees the livelihood of female babies. Today, though, most people are not aware of this need for two ceremonies and typically just have the one Kinaaldá ceremony.

The next time the basket plays an important ceremonial role in a person's life is during the Navajo wedding ceremony. It is from this ceremony, probably witnessed most often by non-Navajos, that the basket derived its nickname, the Navajo wedding basket. The basket is a symbol of their future life being put into the basket—it is safeguarded by the basket. My friend, Jenelia Benally, looks to her own ceremonial basket for strength in facing the demands of marriage and family. She remembers the promises and responsibilities laid out during her wedding when she looks at her basket. According to June Blackhorse, after a woman is married, she should get washed in that basket, and after she is washed, she is purified and can have a baby.

The ceremonial basket will come into play again and again over the course of a person's life as the need for various ceremonies arises. Peggy Black and her husband, Eddie, are both fine weavers of baskets and deeply involved in traditional ways. Eddie is an herbalist and is studying with his uncle and grandfather, both medicine men, so that he too may be a medicine man. Peggy is a prolific weaver, depicting contemporary renditions of traditional themes. Though she lives in a house, she often weaves her baskets in a hooghan nearby. When Peggy started weaving, she realized it was a part of life because she was making her baskets for other people. She knows the significance and importance of the basket.

On this particular day, Peggy talked about her need for a Beauty Way ceremony, a rite she has once each year to keep herself in balance. She is having headaches lately and is feeling the need for the ceremony. However, her ceremony must be postponed until Eddie can have a Ghost Way. He had seen someone die in front of him and he needed to have his ceremony first before Peggy has her Beauty Way. Eddie's ceremony lasts five days and he will need three baskets for the ceremony: one to hold the jish (medicine bundles), one for the herbs, and one for the ritual bathing.

Basket artist, Peggy Black, near the Navajo Pavilion at the 2002 Winter
Olympics with her specially woven Winter Olympics basket.

Peggy also talked about the basket's use in straightening out a person's mind.
My favorite metaphor for the basket, in fact the motivational symbol I used
throughout the creation of this book, is the idea of using the basket to "turn your
mind right." When someone leaves the reservation for a long time, for example a
soldier serving duty overseas, upon returning to the reservation, it is necessary to
"twist the mind back into the reservation." In this simple ceremony, the basket is
turned in a clockwise direction. No matter how far the person has wandered from
traditional ways, practical thinking, and peaceful living, the goal of this ceremony
is to unwind the problems and bring the person back into balance. Peggy summed

it up in this manner: "With us Navajo, there is always something there where we can be healed and we can find out. I feel people need to know so they know how to heal."

Clayton Long, bilingual coordinator for San Juan School District in southern Utah, is responsible for Navajo culture and language instruction throughout the schools. Clayton loves languages, a feeling born from his early struggles mastering English as a second language. In the spring of 2002 he taught a Navajo language class in which I was one of his students. Clayton is one of the most innovative and generous instructors I have encountered. He consistently wove into our instruction the Navajo philosophy of balance and harmony typically portrayed in groups of four: the sacred mountains, the directions, the time of day, the thought processes that occur throughout the day, and the sacred colors—white, blue, yellow, and black. Each of these concepts is centered around and strengthened by prayer.

A year later, while sitting in his office finalizing the glossary for this book, I happened to glance up at his wall and spot an image of an unusual ceremonial basket, one with a typical center. The rim, however, was woven with the four sacred colors. Upon closer inspection, I realized it was a visual aid demonstrating the concept Clayton had so carefully and thoroughly overlayed throughout our instruction. He explained that he had a basket artist named Alice Grey Mountain weave the basket, and then he built a handout around all of the things that anchor Navajo people during each day of their lives. It perfectly depicts Clayton's approach to his own life, and provides a meaningful guide for any person, Navajo or otherwise, to follow.

Dibé Nitsaa
v

"With strong self-confidence I have hope for a better tomorrow."

Sih Hwiinzin

"My beautiful creative Thoughts give me direction."

Sisnaajiní

Ntsáhákees

Sodizin
Sin

Iiná

Dook'o'oosłííd

"Implementing my thoughts and planning allows me to live Hózhóogo Iiná."

Nahat'á

"My beautiful Planning from beginning to the end makes my Dreams come true."

Tsoodził

Clayton Long's handout.

6. Sacred Space

The People were created in the underground worlds. They emerged from the center in this Fourth World which we call the Glittering World and started journeying. When the Holy People finished teaching the people in this world, they wanted to go to a resting place which is represented by the four sacred mountains, plus the Huerfano where Changing Woman (Asdzą́ą́ Nádleehé) resides as well as Navajo Mountain. These six mountains are where the Holy People reside. It is also why the hooghan is six-sided. In order to preserve the history and language of the people, protection was needed which is represented by the red rainbow design in the basket. Next is Father Sky and the clouds which represent the nourishment needed to keep the culture going. Finally, the braiding at the rim is protection so the Navajo people won't forget from where they came.

Geno Bahe

Every ceremonial basket conveys a similar metaphor. Jack Rock, father of basket maker Charlene Rock, emphasized the importance of leaving a tiny opening at the start of each basket. He said, "You don't want to close the place of emergence."A Navajo person who may not be well versed in the history of the basket still often possesses a basic understanding of its symbolism and capabilities for providing

protection. To understand the basket's ceremonial role, one must first understand
the need for ceremony. Charlotte Frisbie, the author of the definitive volume on
Navajo jish (medicine bundles), eloquently explains this concept.

> When one ignores the prescriptions and the constant warnings from the
> Holy People which are relayed by Messenger Winds, or precipitates an
> imbalance by indulging in excesses, having improper contact with dan-
> gerous powers, or deliberately or unwittingly breaking other rules—con-
> flict, disharmony, disorder, evil, sickness of the body and mind, ugliness,
> misfortune and/or disaster (Hóchx̨ǫ—evil) result. Consequently, the
> appropriate traditional action is first to have a family-level conference to
> consider the possible causes of the sickness. After this, the person can also
> turn to diagnosticians among the Navajos—hand-tremblers, stargazers, or
> listeners—for further diagnosis and suggestions about ritual steps neces-
> sary to rectify matters. Such steps usually involve having a ceremony
> designed to deal with the etiology of the illness (including infection by
> animals, natural phenomena, ceremonials, and evil spirits [both ghosts
> and witches], according to Wyman and Kluckhohn [1938:13-15]), and to
> involve the relevant supernaturals in the restoration/healing of the suffer-
> ing person. These ceremonials work simultaneously in the physical, men-
> tal, spiritual, and social realms, with the goal of reinstituting harmony in
> all environments. (Frisbie, 1985:4)

Basket making is an arduous process that begins with the gathering of materials for making the basket. Sumac (*Rhus trilobata*) is the principle material used in
the making of Navajo baskets. Weavers sometimes travel long distances in order to
locate good plants. Evelyn Cly, a well-known weaver of fine ceremonial baskets,
speaks about the trials of gathering sumac.

> I only gather my materials in the fall. Sumac (chiiłchin) is nice in the fall.
> If you gather in the summer, the willow is brittle. I go as far as Green
> River, Utah, a three hour drive. You don't necessarily cultivate the sumac.
> How much sumac I gather depends on how much I am able to find. I have
> to get BLM (Bureau of Land Management) permits to gather the sumac.
> and they charge me according to the size of the vehicle, usually around ten
> dollars. I have to go to the Moab BLM office on my way to Green River.
> There are some other places closer to home, but the last two years there has
> been limited access. The sumac has to be processed immediately. It takes
> about a week to ten days to split all of the sumac into weaving strands.
> Rods are just wrapped in plastic so they don't dry out. I split the weaving

Sumac, *Rhus trilobata*, chiiłchin.

strips and hang them in the bathroom so I don't use it until I am ready to
weave. (Evelyn Cly, interview by the author, February 28, 2001)

When gathering materials, the weaver will bless a nearby sumac plant with corn
pollen without cutting any of its branches. Their offering shows gratitude toward
the plants in allowing them to take part of it away for the making of this important
ceremonial item. They will proceed to cut long, straight sumac branches from other
surrounding plants, being careful to never take too much from any one plant. The
cut sumac is considered to be sacred and therefore must be stored where it won't be
tampered with.

The weaving of a basket starts with a thought in the artist's head. "Right
thinking" is crucial if the weaver is going to properly execute the basket. Certain

prescriptions and procedures must be followed or the basket will be flawed. For example, the rules of butts and tips apply to the making of a basket. Specifically applied here, when a weaver initiates the coil in a basket, she must start with the butt end of a rod, meaning the end growing closest to the ground when cut. Whenever, the weaver adds a new rod, it must be inserted in this same manner, never the tip of the branch. This organic process follows the philosophy that the basket is growing out and you are following the natural pattern of the sumac and in a larger sense, the pattern of nature itself, by inserting it in this fashion. The creation of a basket is not taken lightly. Martina Cly, a young weaver who learned basket making from her mother, Evelyn, considers herself an artist, someone who makes things using her thoughts, and puts her mind into it. In getting ready to make the basket, she thinks about how it will be designed. She won't sit down to weave if her mind is on other things such as schoolwork or chores. This concept of "right thinking" is not unusual among Native American artists. They know that the creation of something beautiful and balanced starts with aligning your thoughts properly before and during the artistic process.

> It takes strong mental thoughts to complete a basket. One needs to think strongly when making a basket. There are many people such as young men and women and adults, who will benefit from the use of the basket in the ceremonies . . . I have spent several winters learning how to make a Navajo basket. Will I learn? Can I ever make a good basket? These are the questions that you ask yourself. It took me several winters to learn how. Now people know I can make baskets and I help them out with the baskets I make. —Connie Tso, Many Farms, AZ, as told to Ruth Roessel, June 20, 1978. Roessel 1983:134

An extremely important aspect in the design construction is the opening, the atiin (road, path), beginning at the center of the basket and moving in a straight line to the edge of the basket, meeting at the exact spot where the weaver terminates her weaving. Maureen Trudelle Schwarz interviewed Flora Ashley of Tsaile, Arizona, regarding this opening. Following are the author's observations, succeeded by Flora's thoughts.

As Flora Ashley explains in what follows, because of the paradigm established by the Diyin Dine'é through their emergence out of the underworlds, the need for a "way out" is universal in the Navajo world. Navajo people must provide a "way out" in all artifacts they manufacture because in the process of construction the artifact becomes both part of its creator and a conduit for creative processes and thoughts. As a result, an artisan who neglects to include a "way out" in an artistic product risks blockage of her or his thinking and creative powers.

> FA: We always have an opening. Because we breathe every day. And we want our artifacts to breathe with us too. And then, they also tell us that somewhere you do it unfinished, like it might have an unfinished place in order that your whole cycle is not done yet.

> MS: What is called the atiin [road], is that the opening?

> FA: This is your path of the life here. If you close it then you are just blocking up your own path. So, there is always a path in every, a passage through everything, because of the emergence. Because we believe there is always another "way out." There is always an "out" somewhere. So, when you make this basket the weave at the end [must be at the opening in the design]. (Schwarz 1997, 108)

The *atiin* is often mentioned in discussions as being a "way out." medicine men John Holiday and June Blackhorse shine a different light on the opening. First, there is the practical aspect of using the design to help orient the basket toward the east during a ceremony. More important, though, is that both men talk about how this opening reflects what happens with all of a person's knowledge at the end of his or her life. When you are reaching the end of your life and you are starting to forget everything, it is as if you return to the same state as when you were a child. Traditional Navajo people do not believe in reincarnation, but they do believe that all of the energy and knowledge from a person's life flows back to the beginning and is there for the next generation.

There used to exist many taboos specific to the making of baskets. In fact, many people feel that these basket making prescriptions became so restrictive that they curtailed weaving among Navajo women. In 1938, Harry Tschopik Jr. wrote an article about taboo and its effect on Navajo pottery and basket weaving. He lists the following restrictions:

> Such taboos included going some distance from the hooghan to work; no one may watch; do not bother snakes or frogs and do not harm dogs or puppies; do not step over the materials used in basket making; do not touch with bloody hands; do not jump across deep ditches; do not swear; stay out of caves, and do not hit another person. A woman must always work on the concave surface of a basket; if she turns it over, she would

lose her mind. She must never allow a child to place sumac (chiiłchin) on his head or else it would stunt his growth. If she works on the basket in a high wind, the materials will split. Should the basket or materials be burned, she would lose her mind. If a man works on a basket, he will become impotent. While a woman is working on a basket, she may not sleep with her husband. While menstruating, she may not work on the basket at all and must purify herself afterwards before she may resume her work. If she is out during a rain, she must walk slowly and may never run. Should she be riding, she must get off her horse until the rain is over. If she neglected to put the doorway in the basketry design, she would lose her mind or else go blind. When the sumac is cut in preparation to making a basket, it must be tied with a yucca leaf, but never with string or anything else. After the design has been started she may eat only a little meat and bread, but no salt. In coiling the basket, the butt end of one rod must be placed next to the top end of the previous rod; the reverse of this situation may never occur, or the basket cannot be used in a "sing." The scraps of the basketry material must be placed in a tree, or under a rock in the shade.

Basket materials never go to waste because great value is placed on the materials. In addition to proper disposal of any leftover materials, another use for the leftover sumac is in the creation of what are called "bugaboo owls," special little protection devices that can be hung in the home. We have several hanging in the trading post and I noticed one hanging in the curator's office at Hubbell Trading Post. June Blackhorse says there are supposed to be four of the owls hanging in the house, one for each of the cardinal directions, but two can be hung oriented to the east and west, or even just one. He smiled and said, "It's a little bit like insurance—the more you have, the better off you are."

Basket making is a difficult undertaking and with the many ritual restrictions, it became nearly impossible for a Navajo woman to weave baskets. Fortunately, these prohibitions did not apply to her Ute and Paiute neighbors. With the Navajo population increasing dramatically around the turn of the twentieth century, and the corresponding increase in demand for ceremonial baskets, it is not surprising that they turned to their neighbors to fill this void. During this same period, the market for rug weaving was increasing, so many Navajo women gravitated toward the more lucrative undertaking of weaving rugs. With the sale of those weavings, they now had the money to pay someone else to make the baskets. A weaver was required to tackle her

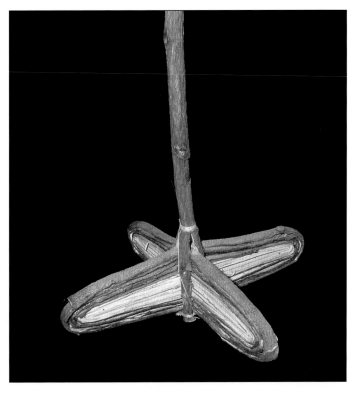

Bugaboo Owl made by Wilson Warren.
—Courtesy of Twin Rocks Trading Post.

basket making with the utmost skill, dedication, and speed. It was believed that if an unskilled weaver attempted to make a basket, or even if a skilled weaver procrastinated in her task, they were inviting sickness, including arthritic stiffness around the wrists, hands, and joints. It was for this reason that Peggy and Eddie Black prodded their daughter, Sonja, to finish her baskets. Sonja would start and then not finish a basket. She was told that she needed to finish what she started or "things will not go on—they will just get cut off. She will not be complete of mind unless she finishes the basket."

A requirement exists that says when approaching the finish of the basket, the rim weaving must be completed in one day. There is a ritual and practical relation to this philosophy as expressed by basket weaver Connie Tso:

> When finishing the top final circle of the basket it is important this be completed in one day. One may need to get up in the early morning so it can be finished in one day. The reason is that when such a basket is used in a ceremony the patient will get well quickly. (Connie Tso, Many Farms, Arizona, as told to Ruth Roessel, June 20, 1978.)

Sonja Black with Ceremonial Variation Basket featuring a rainbow yé'ii.

Several references state that if the rim finish is worn or torn, the basket is unfit for ceremonial use. For some practitioners this holds true, but in John Holiday's case, he will sprinkle corn pollen on the break to, in essence, "seal" the perimeter of the basket. When deemed useless for ceremonial purposes, a basket is not discarded carelessly but rather safely placed in the fork of a tree above where sheep or other livestock cannot trample or chew on the basket. The basket is always treated with the greatest respect. Another aspect of the rim finish is that the end of it must align with the opening of the basket design break from the center. This practical requirement, along with the design break in the black and red elements, allows the medicine man to properly orient the basket's opening to the east even under the poorest lighting conditions.

The special restrictions in the construction of the basket paired with the deep symbolism behind the design set the foundation for a ritual place, a sacred space within the confines of the basket. The creation of the basket permeates a certain "personhood" into the basket.

> Rug, sandpainting, and basket persons, like looms, cradles, and hooghan, are initially imbued with life by their makers during the process of construction. On the basis of the principle of synechdoche, this process forms an inalienable connection between maker and product. Moreover, as Harry Walters points out, an individual artifact can take on a life of its own through use in a ceremonial context. For, as Harry Walters noted, artifacts, such as the basket in his example, acquire "a life of their own" when they are imbued with knowledge through the process of being used in a ceremonial context. Navajo persons, have personal power based on knowledge, which gives them agency and volition. They have power and agency because they are Navajo persons, who are integral to ceremonial healing. Things made for a ritual purpose are imbued with power and agency because the process of their construction "represents a ceremonial order . . a history." (Harry Walters, interviewed by Schwarz 1997, 53)

Once the basket moves off of the reservation, however, it is believed that this "personhood" cannot survive. It can be re-imbued, so to speak, simply by being returned to a ceremonial setting where the characteristics needed for protection and blessing during the ceremony are reestablished.

The power of the basket is to be respected. It is used for healing. John Holiday spoke of the duality of the basket. He said, "Like us, the basket has two spirits. We are both male and female and our heart marries us." He went on to say that the basket, if it is for a man, is called "Many Farms," and if it is for a woman, it is called "Making of the Cornfield." Harry Walters also expresses the double nature of the basket, the fact that it embodies both the male and female, the warrior and the peacemaker. It is the peaceful side that is summoned for healing, but the warrior side is needed to provide strength and protection. (Harry Walters, interview by Schwarz

Evelyn Cly Ceremonial Basket.

1997, 54-55) This philosophy is important when the basket is used for protecting any of its contents during a ceremony. Mother Earth is thought to possess great power, an energy that emanates up toward an individual or other objects, especially during a ceremony. For this reason, ritual paraphernalia is never placed directly on the ground but rather often placed in a basket for protection and safekeeping. Also, people attending a ceremony need to be clear of thought and conscience while attending in order to provide the most benefit to the patient. Unfortunately, some individuals may attend who are malevolent toward the patient to such an extent that it can harm the individual and the ceremonial proceedings. By placing objects in the basket, a shield is provided against any dark thoughts that may be directed toward the ritual paraphernalia.

The number of baskets required for a ceremony is dependent on the type of ceremony and a prearranged agreement with the medicine man as to the number necessary for that ceremony. It typically ranges from one to seven baskets, with the larger number needed for the longer ceremonies lasting from five to nine days. For example, it is typical at a wedding ceremony to have two baskets, one for the sacred mush to be consumed by the wedding couple and another to hold jewelry and other treasured possessions. This same number holds true for the Kinaaldá, as one is used for holding the sacred meal and for ritual bathing, while another holds jewelry and other possessions of the initiate. My friend, Allison Billy, is having an important ceremony performed for him in March. He needs to find three baskets woven in a clockwise direction.

The direction a basket is woven typically is determined by whether a basket weaver is right- or left-handed; a right-handed weaver will weave a counter-clockwise coil while the opposite is true of a left-handed weaver. Few clockwise baskets are made although it is often preferred for ceremonies as the coil winds in accordance with the passage of time. There are weavers who are able to execute their basket weaving in either direction. A person needing baskets will either approach a weaver or go to the local trading post to purchase the baskets. Trading posts and pawn shops play an important role as a repository for baskets. Evelyn Cly, Peggy Black's sister, is particularly focussed on making ceremonial baskets and creates some of the nicest, most well-balanced ceremonial baskets woven today. Evelyn remembers that if there was a ceremony needed for someone in the family on her mom's side, everyone would weave their own in order to have the baskets for the ceremony instead of going out and buying baskets. For example, they recently made seven baskets that were used in a ceremony. They put different herbs in each basket. Sometimes they would only find out the day before a ceremony that a basket was needed and they would have to make the basket in one day.

The importance of ceremony in a Navajo person's life is amusingly illustrated in an encounter between Navajo basketmaker, Peggy Black, and my brother-in-law, Barry. Peggy is a tremendous artist, creating some of the most dynamic baskets woven today. She is firmly grounded in her beliefs to the extent that regular cere-monies are important in maintaining her overall health as well as her ability to con-tinue weaving. Barry relates this story:

> "One day Peggy brought in a gorgeous basket with a profusion of Yé'ii figures. I was pleased with its creativity and visual appeal. So, I cracked open the volumes of past knowledge and began comparing its size, weave and creative appeal. Thereafter, I proudly proclaimed a price I felt was compatible with her previous works. Peggy simply looked at me with her sad eyes, shaking her head as if showing complete disillusionment with

The strong, stained hands of Navajo basket weaver, Peggy Black.

one of her "slower" pupils. Wincing under "that look," I asked, "Where have I gone wrong? I have done my homework, studied hard, and learned my lessons well. I even have a degree in "Trading Postology!" Peggy looked at me as if enduring unbearable hardship and began to explain, "When I weave the Yé'ii Bicheii, I am portraying extremely sacred and powerful beings—ones that demand respect. If I convey this respect in the proper manner, these Holy People will bless me and my family. If I show disrespect, these same beings can, and will, cause me much trouble. One way I show that respect, and protect myself from harm, is by having a Beauty Way ceremony done each year. I save part of the price from each basket to pay for the ceremony. Since you are involved, you too must help keep me safe and healthy." (Barry and Steve Simpson)

Now, this may appear to be a very clever device for raising the price of her basket if you did not know Peggy and the extent of her sincerity. Ceremony is as necessary to her being as breathing. She fully understands the balance and protection it brings to her life. Ceremonies range from one to nine days. As mentioned, the number of baskets needed is determined by the type of ceremony and the requirements of the medicine man conducting the ceremony. Many ceremonies have become extinct in the past century. Medicine man, June Blackhorse, listed a few that are still held today including the two nine day ceremonies, the Yé'ii Bicheii and the Mountain Top Way (Dziłk'ihjí). The basket is used in a variety of ways throughout these ceremonies, plus there is a very special basket made especially for the Fire Dance (Mountain Top Way or Dziłk'ihjí). The categories of use for the basket fall into these main areas: the basket tray as a receptacle for medicine, sacred objects, and ritual paraphernalia; a protected space for personal belongings; a container of sacred meal; for ceremonial bathing; as a ceremonial headdress; and as a sacred and highly specialized drum.

The Basket as a Receptacle for Sacred Objects and Ritual Paraphernalia

When Eddie Black, Peggy's husband and a basket artist in his own right, recently required a ceremony, he undertook weaving the baskets needed for a ceremony Peggy labeled Ghost Way. He said he needed three baskets: one to hold the jish (medicine bundle); one to hold herbs; and one for bathing. The ceremonial basket serves as a protected place for sacred items needed throughout a ceremony. For example, in certain ceremonies where a sweat lodge is required, turkey feathers are placed outside of this lodge. The turkey feathers are carried to the location in a ceremonial basket to ensure no evil contaminates them on their way. After the sweating is completed, the feathers are gathered back into the basket and carried into the medicine lodge.

In Charlotte J. Frisbie's comprehensive volume, *Navajo Medicine Bundles or Jish,* she recounts numerous situations where the basket is used for holding medicine paraphernalia. In fact, on one occasion, Frank Mitchell, one of the medicine men with whom she worked extensively, agreed to be filmed by David P. McAllester. The filming took place in 1957 and the following is McAllester's account as related to Charlotte Frisbie in a private conversation in 1979:

> After these things were laid out roughly, two baskets were brought up and
> set on the white cloth; one was placed in about the center, on the north end
> of the buckskin strip; the other one, north of that, rested on the cloth next to

where the protagonist was sitting. On the second night, this second basket remained shrouded in some kind of cover (possibly a very fine buckskin loosely wrapped around it). On the first night the cover was removed to show that the basket served as a container for several long, slim pouches. The other basket, at about the center of the cloth strip, had several pouches in it. (Frisbie, 65)

The two wedding baskets were part of Frank Mitchell's Blessingway equipment because along with everything else contained in his medicine bundles, he felt the baskets were representative of all the items included in the original jish of First Man. There are several ways in which jish may be organized with the "basket layout" being one of the options.

One of the ways in which jish are ceremonially employed is in displays or "layouts." As Reichard (ibid.,) indicates, there are at least four possibilities: spread layout, basket layout, set out mound, and set-up. The start of some indoor ceremonials is signified by spreading, or laying, out relevant jish contents in an order determined by the sex of the one sung over. These are positioned on a buckskin, calico, or other kind of cloth that has been placed in the west of the hooghan, in front of or between the singer (hataałii) and one-sung-over. (Kluckhohn and Wyman 1940, 59-60) term this the spread layout. If a sandpainting is to be made, jish contents are put in a basket. While the singer usually opens the jish and lays out the equipment, during antelope hunting, at the start of the all-night Blessingway after the construction of the antelope corral, the leader chooses two people to open, unwrap, and finally, rewrap the medicine bundle (which contains male and female bluebirds). (Hill 1948, 150; Frisbie, 114)

Another important role for the basket is holding the k'eet'áán, the prayersticks, for ritual sacrifice during various ceremonies. During the day, helpers will assist the medicine man in assembling the needed k'eet'áán. Washington Matthews made extensive observations of their preparation and proper storage:

> Like other sacred articles these kethawn [k'eet'áán] must not touch the ground while being prepared. They must be laid on clean cloths or buckskins which must, in turn, be laid on blankets. When a finished kethawn [k'eet'áán] is placed in the basket, the point must be in the east and the breath-feather must hang over the edge of the basket. . . . It takes about an hour to prepare the kethawns [k'eet'áán], several men working on them at the same time. When done they are placed one on top of another in one or more sacred baskets (I have seen them once divided into three groups, each

group in a separate basket) to await the preparation of the actors who are to handle them. (Matthews 1995, 68)

The basket containing the finished kethawns [k'eet'áán] is put to one side, in the mask recess or other secure place, where it is kept until needed at night. (Matthews 1995, 93-94)

Fire Dance painting by Navajo artist, Jimmy Toddy, circa 1950.
—Photo courtesy of the U.S. Department of the Interior, Indian Arts and Crafts Board, Southern Plains Indian Museum, William and Leslie Van Ness Denman Collection.

Dziłk'ihjí—Mountain Top Way (Fire Dance)

This brings us to the story of the Fire Dance basket. I grew up with a particular painting hanging in our home by well-known Navajo artist, Beatin Yazz, depicting the Fire Dance, the spectacular performance that culminates the Mountain Top Way ceremony. I would often find myself staring at the image, fascinated by the wild dancing with flames from the torches licking the dancers' bodies. Later in life, it came to my attention that this particular ceremony was in danger of extinction. Fortunately, in the last few years, I have noticed signs announcing the ceremony in various locations throughout the reservation.

The ceremony does not necessarily take place on top of a mountain, but should still be conducted in some location with a higher elevation whether it be a mountain or mesa top. It invokes the spirit of such mountain animals as the bear, snake, porcupine and weasel. It is supposed to be conducted during the winter months at a time that falls between the first frost of winter and the first thunder of spring. It is during this time that stories of the animals can be told, whether in this ceremony or perhaps during a shoe game, the time when especially the bear and snake are hibernating. I have seen signs during the summer advertising a Fire Dance. Supposedly, a shorter, five-day version can be performed during this time. According to Caroline B. Olin, the purpose of this ceremony is for the restoration of good and typically includes sandpaintings with the first four days consisting of blessing rites and preparation of various kinds. The next four days are reserved for the construction of sandpaintings, leaving the final day and night for special dances and events. There are examples of sleight of hand that happen during this last night, including a particular illusion my father, John Kennedy, remembers seeing performed at a Fire Dance he attended as a teenager in the 1920s. It involves a medicine man enticing a feather to "dance" on a ceremonial basket. Betty Yazzie also mentioned this particular phenomenon and short references to it appear in the text of the Franciscan Fathers (pages 377-8).

> This chant is sung to treat mental troubles or uneasiness ("Bear sickness"), fainting spells and to cure diseases and infections attributed to mountain animals (kidney and stomach troubles). In the first sandpainting (constructed on the fifth day of the ceremony), the Black Mountain Sandpainting, four figures are depicted: the Male Black Bear; Female White Bear; the Male Thunder; and the Female Big Chipmunk. Among other ritual paraphernalia that each figure holds, each figure holds a basket in its left hand. This basket contains a rainbow inside and a string attached to a sprig of fir, the end of which is fixed for putting into the medicine pouch to feed the patient. Feathers are placed on the basket when the medicine man begins to sing. (Olin 1982, 132)

When I was first showing June Blackhorse the images of older baskets woven about a century before, he noticed one design and started talking about a special little basket made specifically for the Fire Dance. He said a medicine man commissions a weaver to create, typically, a small basket approximately five inches across

Fire Dance ceremonial
basket, circa 1950.

(although it can be larger or smaller in size). The practitioner then takes four strings
and attaches them to the basket to align with the four directions and ties four feathers to each of the strings. This special basket holds medicine during the ceremony.

I was certain I would never see such a basket. A few months ago, I received a
phone call from an acquaintance. A grandson of a medicine man who had practiced
in an area just south of Bluff had brought him a basket and he didn't know what to
make of it. As he started describing the basket to me, I grew excited with the realization that it was this special basket of the Fire Dance. This particular little basket
is a thing of beauty, nicely woven and approximately fifty years old. It is the only
other basket tray of which we are aware outside of the traditional ceremonial basket that is woven specifically for use in ceremony.

Protected Space for Personal Belongings

A number of individuals with whom I visited talk about a particular secular use of the basket within the home in which personal belongings are placed in the basket for protection and blessing. It is not unusual for a family's jewelry or other prized possessions to be stored in a basket within the home for safekeeping. The feeling is that while any of their personal belongings are within the confines of the basket, no outsider can imbue them with ill feelings or thoughts. This type of use crops up over and over with the same basic objective of protecting any items within the confines of the basket. In a *Navajo Times* article dated September 27, 2001, there is a wonderful image by staff photographer, Paul Natonabah, showing the badges of a retired Navajo police officer placed in a ceremonial basket. The image immediately communicates that the badges are prized and worthy of special protection. Maureen Trudelle Schwarz conveys in her book, *Molded in the Image of Changing Woman,* an example of when one family was holding a Blessingway ceremony, photographs of family members who could not attend were placed in the ceremonial basket with the jish. (Thomas, interviewed by the author, January 21, 1995; Schwarz 1997, 259) During several conversations, different informants spoke about the need of the basket for protecting and blessing prized personal items during a ceremony. Although all those attending a ceremony for an individual are supposed to be there with good thoughts and energy directed at the patient, sometimes the opposite is true and therefore, it is necessary to have your most prized personal possessions ensconced in a basket to keep any evil intentions at bay.

Sacred Meal, Mush, and Other Foods

My first experience witnessing the basket's use as a container of sacred mush was during a Navajo wedding ceremony. This particular ceremony is witnessed more often by non-Navajo people than any other ceremony and is probably the reason why the ceremonial basket earned the nickname "wedding basket." Wedding ceremonies are performed slightly differently depending on the way a family has learned this particular ritual. In our area, the ceremony typically takes place at the bride's family home and the bride is responsible for bringing a basket for the ceremony. The father or another male relative of the bride is responsible for conducting the ceremony. After the wedding guests are seated, he typically enters first carrying a pitch basket (tóshjeeh) or other vessel filled with water. The bride then enters carrying a wedding basket filled with sacred mush. The man leading the ceremony takes sacred corn pollen and creates a cross over the meal starting at the eastern edge of the basket and crossing west; then from south to north, then starting at the east drawing a nearly complete circle of pollen around the perimeter of the mush. June Blackhorse spoke of the symbolism of this gesture saying that the east-west line represents the boy children to be born and the south-north line symbolizes the female children to be born. A child is represented at each directional point of the sacred pollen, plus where the two lines intersect in the middle. In essence, this ritual provides blessings for five children in the marriage. He said it is analogous to the five fingers of your hand, in effect, that you are offering a helping hand to the young couple. I noticed in several descriptions where the practitioner crosses over and back when applying the corn pollen, in essence, east-west-east and south-north-south. June said that this should not be done as it is akin to giving the blessing, then taking it away. The groom then proceeds to take some mush from each of the five points. He starts by dipping his fingertips into the mush at the eastern point of the corn pollen and is followed by the bride dipping and consuming the meal from the same place. He, then proceeds to each of the points in a sunwise direction-south, west, north, then center with the bride taking her corresponding fingerful each time after the groom.

> The reason that they take the cornmeal from the four directions is because you are saying that, "All the knowledge that lies to the east, we want that in our marriage. All the knowledge that lies in the south, we want that in our marriage. All the knowledge to the west, all the knowledge to the north." And where the pollen crosses in the center—the direction from the east to west is male, the direction from the north to south is female. And then so, when you take you know, pinches [of] the cornmeal from where the male and female [lines of pollen] cross, it is for the children that you are going to have. The grandchildren, the great-grandchildren you are going to have. That is what it signifies. (Harry Walters, interviewed by Schwarz 1997, 71-72)

The girl's parents then consume meal from the basket. Some say it should be the groom's parents, but June did not feel this to be correct as it is the woman who traditionally provides food for the family. Finally, everyone attending the ceremony consumes meal from the basket until it is depleted. The basket is then given to the groom's mother. In effect, by her holding the basket, she is responsible for the

Older ceremonial baskets featuring plug and cornmeal packed into grooves.
—Courtesy Simpson Family Private Collection.

safekeeping of the marriage. She must protect that basket in order to protect the bonds of the marriage itself.

When my husband, Steve, and I were married, instead of getting a ring, I asked for a wedding basket. Knowing full well my active and hectic lifestyle, I knew a ring would most likely end up down a drain or trampled in the horse corral. In this way, I have the basket safely ensconced in our home and I can look upon it every day and be reminded of our promise to each other. I suppose, however, if I were to be truly traditional about it, I should have handed the basket over to my mother-in-law, Rose.

In preparing a basket to hold sacred meal or medicines, it is common practice to make the basket water-tight. Before a ceremony is to begin, the medicine man will soak the basket in water in order for the coils and weft stitches to expand and therefore close some of the gaps in the basket. A plug is often placed into the emergence spot to prevent leakage there. After soaking the basket, cornmeal is packed into its grooves to further seal it. With the invention of plastic cling wrap, it is not unusual for a basket to be sealed and protected in this manner. The family owners of the Kin łichíi'nii basket use this method because they wish to prevent wear and tear to their basket as much as possible.

During the Night Chant ceremony, there is a time where baskets filled with many types of traditional foods are placed around a fire in the medicine hooghan.

The medicine man will take a pinch of food from each of the baskets and place it into another basket. The combined food is then blessed and made into a powerful medicine by the practitioner. At other times during a ceremony, the patient may be required to take sacred corn meal from a basket and sprinkle it on prescribed places in a sandpainting. During times when the yé'ii perform, the invalid will hold a basket and sprinkle meal on each of the dancers.

Yé'ii Bicheii representation including medicine man and patient with sacred meal basket.
—Carved by Clitso Dedman.
—Image courtesy of California Academy of Sciences, San Francisco, California, the Ruth and Charles Elkus Collection; catalog # CAS 0370-0503 A to P; Photo by Dong Lin.

James Stevenson in his ethnographic report about the Night Chant sums up the use of the basket throughout the ceremony in the following manner. "On the sixth day a great sandpainting is made in the medicine lodge, and the invalid, as he enters, is required to take the sacred medicine basket, which is now filled with sacred meal, and sprinkle the painting with it. The chief figures of the painting were the goddesses of the rainbow, whose favor it was desired he should gain. Again and again in the ceremonies these sacred baskets are used, and on the ninth day in the concluding dance the invalid takes it full of sacred meal and sprinkles all the dancers." (Stevenson 1891, 263, 270) Also, at the conclusion of a ceremony, after the last sandpainting has been destroyed, a basket of cornmeal is placed on a blanket in the center of the hooghan. After the cornmeal is blessed, the patient is brought in and after singing is completed, is fed mush by the medicine man from the four sides of the basket, after which the hataałii and patient proceed to finish the mush in the basket. (Klah 1942, 34-35) It is as if the medicine man is saying, "We have gone through this thing together and I am helping you and supporting you on your path to better health."

Medicines are often prepared in the basket. An example is the creation of dah ts'os, or frost medicine. Dah ts'os means simply hoarfrost, but it is also a name of a preparation used for fevers that is supposed to contain all the virtues and cooling properties of frost. Often this is called azee' dah'ts'os or frost medicine. It must be prepared by a virgin. She grinds meal and puts it in a sacred basket. She takes this out before sunrise on a frosty morning, places it under one or more plants and shakes frost crystals into it until it is moist enough for her purpose. She works the moistened meal into a dough, which she carries home before the sun rises and puts it away where the sun cannot shine on it. (Matthews 1995, 46)

Ceremonial Bathing

Ceremonial bathing is another important function of the basket. At a young woman's puberty ceremony, her Kinaaldá, she will ask another individual to support and guide her through the ceremony. This other individual is known as the Ideal Woman, the embodiment of the perfect Navajo woman. Interestingly, I know of a young man who was selected for this honor because in the views of the young female initiate, he embodied the personal traits she wished to incorporate into her own life: kindness; a gentle spirit; generosity; a curious intellect; and an interest in traditional ways. It was somewhat controversial and perhaps a bit confusing for him to serve in this particular position, but the initiate and her family were very happy with their choice. It may be a sign of the times that this person will one day be known as the Ideal Person. Before a young woman is dressed for the first day of ceremony, she has her hair washed in yucca root suds mixed in a ceremonial basket and brushed with a traditional rabbitbrush hairbrush.

Ceremonial bathing is yet one more way in which people purify themselves and ritually rid themselves of any evil or toxins. Washington Matthews provides a very complete accounting of the entire procedure:

> One or two men collect for the "platter" the necessary mud, which must come from the centre of a cultivated field or alkali flat. Naturally moist earth

must be sought. This earth signifies mud taken from the centre of water, as from a drying pond. . .

The rites within the lodge, connected with the bath of soap-root, are usually begun about noon, but they have been seen delayed as late as 3 pm. When all is ready, the patient enters the lodge and sits, in the south or southwest, facing the east, while the chanter forms on the ground to the west of the fire, a circular object, about two feet in diameter, called by the Navahoes thaa'kis; which might here be called, in order to be graphic, a "mud pie," but, to be more elegant, will be called a mud platter, or simply a platter. He spreads on the floor a layer of mud of the size mentioned, and nearly encircles it with a mud rim about three inches high, leaving an opening in the east. He lays on the platter thus formed, from centre to circumference, four spreading spruce branches which almost conceal it. At the first ceremony he ever performs he makes these branches point to the four cardinal points; at the next ceremony he directs them to the intermediate points, and thus he continues to alternate them through his professional career. Some shamans use five spruce branches, putting one in the centre. (In an account by Hasteen Klah, he refers to them as fir branches; June Blackhorse says pinon branches are appropriate.)

Having completed the platter, the chanter takes a Navajo basket of the kind known as the basket-drum (ceremonial basket), puts pollen on its margin, leaving a hiatus in the east, and lays it to the south of the platter with its line of orientation pointing to the east. Into the basket he puts spruce twigs, and then the ingredients for making kétłoh (lotions created for external use during a healing ceremony), or tsoltsin (tólástsiin). A young boy, or girl, assistant pours water into the basket; he waves one cupful from the east, another from the south, another from the west, a fourth from the north, a fifth from the zenith, and after this he puts in the required amount without ceremony. An adult assistant of the same sex as the patient now stirs the mixture. This infusion is for application to the body after the yucca suds; but it is not always made on this occasion—the suds are sometimes washed off with water only.

At this time, too, the cold detergent solution of amole, or soap-root is prepared. A Navajo water-tight basket-drum (ceremonial basket) is laid down near the middle of the lodge, duly oriented; meal is sprinkled on its margin in the usual way; the four small pieces of yucca first cut from the plants are

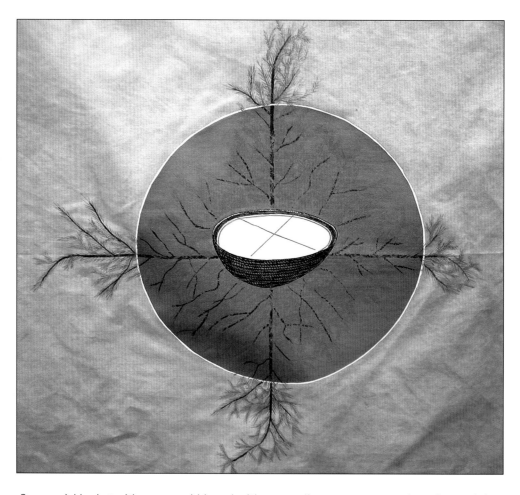

Ceremonial basket with corn meal blessed with corn pollen atop evergreen branches and the "mud platter." Image from Dennis Hathale.
—Courtesy of Georgiana Kennedy Simpson Private Collection.

laid in the bottom of the basket; the rest of the yucca root, or amole, is put in; water is added in the same manner as with the mixture of tsoltsin (tólástsiin), and an assistant, sitting south of the basket bowl and facing north, begins to work up the lather. A high, stiff, lasting lather is produced by whirling in the solution a beater of spruce twigs between the hands as a hand-drill is twirled. The moment the assistant begins to make the foam the shaman begins to sing. The song and the work cease simultaneously. The songs sung on this occasion are the first and second of the Tsalye' Bigi'n (tł'éé'jí biyiin), or Darkness Songs. When the suds are ready, the chanter sprinkles pollen on the rim of the platter sunwise, leaving a hiatus in the east, and places the basket of suds (or an assistant may do this) in the centre of the platter, on top of the butts of the spruce twigs. Pollen is applied to the rim of the oriented basket, leaving an opening in the east. Three superimposed circles of pollen are made around the edge of the suds and three superimposed crosses of pollen are drawn on it from edge to edge. The first line of each cross is drawn from east to west through the centre of the bowl; the second line from south to north. The first circle and cross are made of water pollen, the second of cat-tail pollen, and the third of corn pollen. (An earlier reference by Washington Matthews describes the water pollen as follows: During the summer rains, in the Navaho land, a fine yellow powder collects on the surface of pools; it is probably the pollen of pine; but the Navahoes seem to think it is a product of the water, call it water-pollen, and collect it for use on special occasions.)

Four crosses in pollen are now made around the mud platter, (similar to the rainbow spots seen by the baskets pictured on page 23.) The patient kneels beside the basket of suds, south of it facing north (or west of it facing east, as once observed). He puts to the ground: first, his right knee on cross 1; second, his left knee on cross 2; third, his right hand on cross 3; fourth, his left hand on cross 4; this brings over the suds his head, which he holds low down. (According to June, rainbow bars, rather than crosses, are used if the patient is a woman. James Stevenson points out in his account of the Night Chant that the patient faces toward the north and the basket is placed in such a manner that the sunlight from the fire opening in the hooghan shines on the basket of suds.) An assistant, who must not be of the same gens as the patient, takes a little suds from the tips and centre of the pollen cross and applies it to the patient's head. He next washes well the patient's hair in the suds. The necklace and jewels of the patient may now be washed and rinsed. The patient washes his own face, feet, lower limbs, trunk (in front), and arms. An assistant washes his back. The suds are emptied into the platter, sometimes over the patient's head, and the basket is rinsed into the platter. The body and head of the patient are rinsed. If ke'tlo (kétłoh) has been made it is now applied to the body, which it covers with wet spruce leaves. The patient turns around sunwise and, without touching the earth, gets on a blanket north and west of the mud platter.

A basket containing a goodly quantity of cornmeal is placed before the patient, who sits on a rug. To the accompaniment of song his essential parts are touched with a little of the meal, each application being made at a designated passage in the song. The patient then rubs meal all over his own body—except the back, where a friend rubs it—while a special song to Estsanatlehi (Asdzą́ą́ Nádleehé—Changing Woman) is sung. . . . (June states here that he rarely sees the second basket with lotion unless the patient is particularly ill.)

Not the jewels of the invalid only, but those of the shaman and assistants are washed on this occasion. In addition to an ordinary washing with suds and a rinsing with water, they are sometimes allowed to lie for a while in the bowl of sacred suds, before the circles and crosses of pollen are applied, and sometimes in the bowl of spruce and tso'ltsin (tólástsiin). (Sometimes, only the jewelry of the patient is washed.)

If the patient be a female, three or four female relations accompany her and sit in the north of the lodge, until their turn comes to make themselves useful. One of these may mix the amole; another may wash the patient's head and necklace with the suds. When the body is being washed, two of the women raise a blanket for a screen, while a third assists the patient to bathe the body and a fourth carries the water or cold infusion behind the screen. After a brief interruption, song is resumed, the screen is lowered and the patient is seen standing, clothed. Afterwards, when the woman rubs meal to her person, the screen is again raised by two of her companions and a third rubs the meal on the patient's back. During all this time, there is no exposure of the patient's person to the men in the lodge. (Matthews 1995, 99-103)

After the bathing is completed, the suds, needles, and sands are carried out and disposed of properly. The bathing serves to remove the disease from the individual and the disease is thus removed outside and away from the patient.

The Cloud People

This morning we awoke to a blanket of fog covering our river valley. I thought to myself, "The Cloud People have come for a visit, laying their soft white blankets over us, blankets filled with the promise of moisture." The landscape has disappeared into soft outlines, slightly shifting shades of grey. Was there a tree over there? Is that a house? Have we lost our attachment to the ground as the bluffs disappear, leaving us in a suspended state?

I have eyes, but, at times, I do not see. This feeling overwhelmed me as another revelation regarding the basket and the Holy Ones dawned on me, unfortunately less like the first light of day and more like a "slap upside the head." For years, I have observed sandpainted figures, looking at them without seeing, without taking in the detail necessary to fully understand who the figures represent. After reading many stories about the Humpback Yé'ii, the Water Sprinkler, and the Fringe Mouth, I found repeated references to a "cloud basket," a headdress particular to these Diyin Dine'é. Recently, Allison Billy had attended a Yé'ii Bicheii dance in Shiprock, Arizona. I asked him if he had observed these three figures during that ceremony. He answered in the affirmative and went on to explain the special headdress each figure wore. Apparently, a ceremonial basket is obtained, then the middle is removed to form the foundation of the headdress. Depending on the yé'ii being represented, particular colors and designs are painted on the inside and outside of the basket, then the appropriate accents are added.

When asking June Blackhorse about these deities, he explained that they are the Cloud People, the yé'ii most responsible for bringing moisture to Dinétah. Their headdress are symbolic of clouds. To learn more, I visited John Torres, the curator at the Museum of Indian Art and Culture. After viewing their main collection of Navajo baskets and pottery, he took me into another special storage room. Opening one cabinet and pulling out a drawer, I came face to face with a wondrous site: the cloud basket headdresses of the Palluche cache dated 1698-1775. They were stunning! The baskets themselves were beautifully woven and the painted colors were still quite vibrant. Several of the baskets still had sticks attached that were supports for other attachments to the headdress. Washington Matthews explains the headdress of the Bighą́ą' ask'idii in great detail.

> The mask is the ordinary blue mask of the Yebaka (Yábiką) with the fringe of hair removed. The crown, like that of Dsahadoldza (zaad doolzhaa'í), consists of a Navajo basket from which the bottom has been removed. On the lower surface, it is painted black to represent a storm-cloud and encircled with a zigzag line to depict lightning on the face of the cloud. Ten quills of the red-shafted woodpecker, radiating from the edge of the crown, symbolize sunbeams streaming out at the edge of the cloud. The god is crowned with the storm-cloud. Arising from the crown are two objects intended to represent the horns of the bighorn. These objects are made of dressed bighorn skin, sewed with yucca fibre and stuffed with bighorn hair or the wool of the domestic sheep. They are

Cloud basket headdress from the Palluche cache.—Courtesy of Museum of Indian Art and Culture.

Fringe Mouth depicted by Navajo artist Ray Lansing.—Courtesy Twin Rocks Trading Post.

painted for the most part blue; but at the base they are black, striped longitudinally with white, and they are encircled with white rings at tip and butt. They are tipped with eagle feathers tied on with white strings. (Matthews 1995, 13-14)

If you remember the story of the origin of ceremony, The Visionary (Bił áhát'íinii) met up and was led off by the Bigháá' ask'idii, the Bighorn Sheep. The brother-in-law who attempted to follow their footprints was finally led to a ledge where they all appeared to step off into thin air. There are many Humpback yé'ii, and they are believed to reside in a canyon north of the San Juan River. They appear on the ninth night of the Night Chant and are considered to be the god of harvest, the god of plenty, and the god of mist. The following was told by a medicine man: "In these days, when the Navahoes are hunting and the weather is too dry, if they kill a Rocky Mountain sheep, they cut out the tripe, clear it of its contents, and slap the moist interior surface against a stone. This act in summer brings rain, and in winter, snow." (Matthews 1995, 13-14)

The other group of yé'ii in this group are known as the Fringe Mouth. There are two types: the Fringe Mouth of the Land, who are depicted with the right side of the body painted red and the left side black, and the Fringe Mouth of the Water who are shown with the right side of the body painted yellow and the left side of the body painted blue. Washington Matthews states that these particular deities are never seen

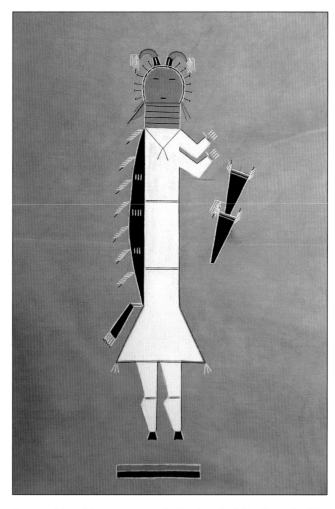

A representation of a cloud headdreass surrounds the head of the figure in this Bigháá' ask'idii. —Humpback Yé'ii painting by Dennis Hathale. —Courtesy of Georgiana Kennedy Simpson Private Collection.

in the dance of the last night, but I have found that to be inaccurate. Allison Billy witnessed them as part of the larger group of yé'ii while attending the Yé'ii Bicheii in Shiprock, New Mexico. Layered above the aforementioned colors were white zigzag lines on the trunk, arms, and legs. These white lines represent lightning, and the yé'ii are believed to carry strings of real lightning, which they use as ropes. There is a circle of coyote hair surrounding their tubular mouth from which their name derives, although there are other gods whose masks demonstrate this feature, too. The crown is painted black on its lower surface with zigzag lines that represent chain lightning. Gladys Reichard stated that the Fringe Mouth represent the "lifting forces of light-

"Fringe Mouth of the Land and Water" painted by Dennis Hathale. Fringe Mouth of the Land is on the left, Fringe Mouth of the Water on the right. The face of each figure is encircled by a cloud basket. —Courtesy of Georgiana Kennedy Simpson Private Collection.

ning." (Reichard 1950, 438) The upper surface of the basket is painted red to represent the sunlight on the back of the cloud. It is bordered with ten tail-feathers of the red-tailed woodpecker to represent rays of sunlight streaming out at the edge of the cloud. Ascending from the basket crown is a tripod of twigs of aromatic sumac (chiiłchin), painted white; between the limbs of the tripod, finely-combed red wool is laid, and a downy feather tips each stick. (Matthews 1995)

James Stevenson provides a slightly different detailed account of the Fringe Mouth:

> These are the Zenichi (Tséníchii'—people of the white rock with a red streak through it) and their wives. Their homes are high in the canyon wall. The black parallelogram to the west of the painting designates a red streak in the rock in which are their homes. The delicate white lines indicate their

Fog Rising Over San Juan River Valley.

houses, which are in the interior or depths of the rock, and cannot be seen from the surface. This canyon wall is located north of the Ute Mountain. These people of the rocks move in the air like birds. The red portion of the bodies of the Zenichi (Tséníchii') denote red corn; the black portion black clouds. The red half of the face represents also the red corn; the blue of the bodies of the others denote vegetation in general, and the yellow, pollen of all vegetation. The zigzag lines of the bodies is lightning; the black lines around the head, zigzagged with white, are cloud baskets that hold red corn, which is stacked in pyramidal form and capped with three eagle plumes. There are five feathers of the red and black shafted flicker in the left hand, the right holds a rattle ornamented with feathers. The females carry in their hands decorated baskets and sprigs of pinon, and they wear white leggings and beaded moccasins. The Zenichi (Tséníchii') never dance. These gods are also called Zaadoljaii (Zaad doolzhaa'í), meaning rough mouth, or anything that protrudes roughly from the mouth. (The mouth and eyes of these gods protrude.) (Stevenson 1891, 265)

Last night, the Cloud People descended once again into our little river valley and the rain fell. The drought-stricken earth accepted their gift and the People rejoiced in their gift. Feelings of quiet and gratitude have enveloped us like the fog. Often their visits are fleeting, but this time, they have decided to spend a few days with us.

The Basket-Drum

Another type of sacred space is created when the basket is "turned down" as a drum. If you have ever held a particularly well made Navajo basket, you will notice how stiff and strong it is, quite a remarkable feat when you consider the suppleness of the materials used. These combined attributes of strength and flexibility render the basket useful as a percussion instrument during certain ceremonies. Hasteen Klah tells of the historic foundation for the basket-drum.

> Now came the fourth night from the time the prophet had descended from the sky. When darkness fell, the yé'ii turned the basket down again to beat time to their singing. They bade the prophet, too, to turn down a basket and recite all the songs he heard. "If you remember them all you may go home in the morning," they said. He put the basket down and began to sing, and the yé'ii outside began to dance as we do now in the dance of the Naakhai' (Na'akai). They then spread a buckskin where the patient had been sitting, and it was a ceremonial one made from a deer that had been caught in a trap and choked to death, no blood being spilled in killing him. They made a small round circle of cornmeal on the buckskin and four lines of corn meal crossing on this circle, then placed a basket on the circle upside down, and folded the buckskin over the basket and called for the patient. The keeper of the drumstick brought it in and sat down on the east side, the patient sitting on the south side of the basket, and they sang six songs, accompanying them with a rattle. . . Begochiddy (Beehoochidii) and Estsan-ah-tlehay (Asdzą́ą́ Nádleehé) told Niltsa-eshki (Níłtsą́ Ashkii) to watch very carefully everything that went on in this ceremony so that he would be able to give it in the future. Then the man with the drumstick struck the basket once from each direction and the holy songs began. . . . They went on singing until the Medicine Man took some coals from the fire and laid them by the patient, sprinkling them with aromatic sumac and making an incense which he inhaled. Then they turned the basket right side up, which completed the ceremony. This singing happened in the evening. (Klah 1946, 27)

A drumstick ritually constructed of yucca is used for beating the drum. During the first four nights of a nine day ceremony, only a rattle is used to accompany singing. On the fifth night, the basket-drum is ritually "turned down." The turning down of the basket is carried out in the following manner during the next five nights.

> For four of these five nights, the following methods are pursued: A small Navajo blanket [or buckskin] is laid on the ground, its longer dimension extending east and west. An incomplete circle of meal, open in the east, of the diameter of the basket, is traced on the blanket near its eastern end. A cross in meal, its ends touching the circle near the cardinal points, is then described within the circle. In making this cross a line is first drawn from east to west, and then a line is drawn from south to north. Meal is then applied sunwise to the rim of the upturned basket so as to form an incomplete circle with its opening in the east. A cross similar to that on the blanket is drawn in meal on the concavity of the basket, the east-and-west line of which cross must pass directly through the hiatus in the ornamental band. The basket is then inverted on the blanket [or buckskin] in such a manner that the figures in meal on the one shall correspond in position to those on the other. The western half of the blanket is then folded over the convexity of the basket and the musicians are ready to begin; but before they begin to beat time to a song they tap the basket with the drumstick at the four cardinal points in the order of east, south, west and north." The Navajos say, "We turn down the basket" when they refer to the commencement of songs in which the basket-drum is used, and "We turn up the basket" when they refer to the ending of the songs for the night. On the last night the basket is turned down with much the same observances as on the previous nights, but the openings in the ornamental band and in the circles of meal are turned to the west instead of to the east, and the eastern half of the blanket is folded over the concavity of the basket. There are songs for turning up and for turning down the basket, and there are certain words in these songs at which the shaman prepares to turn up the basket by putting his hand under its eastern rim, and other words at which he does the turning. For four nights, when the basket is turned down, the eastern part is laid on the outstretched blanket first and it is inverted toward the west. On the fifth night it is inverted in the opposite direction. When it is turned up, it is always lifted first at the eastern edge. (Matthews 1995, 60-61)

The special drum songs are sung in order to collect and trap evil forces under the basket. If at some point during the night, the medicine man turns the basket up before the completion of the basket-drum songs, it signals an end to the ceremony. It presents a dire time during the ceremony because the medicine man is indicating that all is not going well or correctly with the ceremony and it must come to an end. Obviously, it is something an individual does not wish to have happen. When the basket-drum is beaten, those assembled are calling to Mother Earth to help expel the evil gathered under the basket during this particular segment of the ceremony. At the end of each night when the drum is turned up, the medicine man blows the imaginary contents of the drum toward the east and upward out of the hooghan's smoke hole. All of the other people present wave their hands in the same direction in order to help drive the evil forces up, out, and away from the patient, the assembled participants and the hooghan. John Holiday added this thought:

> In ceremony, when you are hitting the drum, that beat goes into the earth. It is telling the gods that evil is going out of the person. On the last night, the worst of the evil goes out. When the basket is turned up, only the good is left.

Basket-drums and the other ceremonial drum made from traditional Navajo pottery, called a water drum, do not exist as permanent instruments in Navajo culture; rather, they are created specifically for ceremonial use. Some believe this is so because the drum has the power to drive away evil forces, therefore making it dangerous to keep. (Franciscan Fathers 1910) Wood and rawhide hand drums have been adopted for use in song and dance performances and have no ritual attachment implied.

7. The Water Jug

I first met Etta sometime in the late 1970s. I was running the forerunner of Twin Rocks Trading Post, which was called Bluff City Trading Post. It was a small hole-in-the-wall that catered to the Navajo people more than the tourists. It was at this upstart business that I met many of the local "colorful characters." Etta is one individual that I place in this category. Needless to say I lost my heart to this quiet, easygoing grandmother. She referred to me as "Duke's boy." Before I knew it, half of my inventory was made up of Etta's pitch pots. "Duke's boy" was about to be disowned by Duke. At one point Etta brought me the largest pitch pot I have ever seen. It was three feet tall and easily as wide. It was the middle of a very hot Bluff summer; sweltering to say the least. Etta and her husband, Jackson, backed up to the front of the old store with a large something wrapped in wet blankets, tied securely in the back of their truck. I began to fidget and wring my hands because my father had threatened me with disastrous consequences if I ever bought another of Etta's "!@#$%" water jars. There was no way out; I was cornered. I was going to have to stand up to Etta or pay the price.

Just then my dear old dad wheeled into the yard. Salvation! I was not too proud to sacrifice my father to Etta's persuasions, to save myself. Both Etta

Etta's monster pitch pot shown with the author's daughter, Kira, and her friend, Summer Bedonie. —Courtesy Georgiana Kennedy Simpson Private Collection.

and my father walked into the store at the same time. I raised my hands, palms facing Etta and said, "No more Etta please." I was thinking that my father was going to go ballistic if I bought more of her pitch pots. Etta turned to Duke and smiled. . . . She turned on the charm, and before you

Etta Rock, basket master.

could say, "There she goes again"' my tough guy dad had been reeled in. It was over quickly. Etta pulled away with a wad of cash, and we became the owners of the largest known pitch pot in the history of the art. I simply looked at my father with mock surprise and said, "What just happened?" Duke just snorted, realizing he had just met a master saleswoman. He walked back outside, climbed into his truck and drove away. From that time forward, whenever I wanted to needle my dear old Dad for one reason or another, I would bring up the monster pitch pot affair. It works beautifully. (Simpson "Etta, Duke, and the Monster Pitch Pot")

One sunny spring afternoon, Allison Billy, my two children, and I headed for the magical landscape of Monument Valley. We were meeting Etta Rock, arguably the best contemporary pitch basket maker. The Navajo pitch basket or tóshjeeh (probably a contraction of tó, water and yishje, it is closed with gum) is a wicker bottle or jar covered with a layer of gum or pitch. (The Franciscan Fathers 1910, 297-298) The pitch basket was most likely adopted from their neighbors, the southern Paiutes. Pitch water vessels are common among the northern and southern Paiute groups. Turning right off

Etta's basket making shed.

of the main highway, we started searching for her pink stucco house. Soon realizing
we were lost, we fortunately spotted the "You Can't Miss Me" yellow truck belonging to two other basket makers, Peter and Elsie Holiday. Stopping to ask directions,
we soon corrected our mistake and went bouncing down the road again. We located
Etta's house and pulled up outside. Her husband, Jackson, stuck his head out the door
and soon Etta appeared at the door wearing a burgundy blouse and grey skirt. She
immediately disappeared back into the house for a few moments.

While we were waiting, my daughter, Kira, climbed out of the car to play with
the puppies skittering about the yard. We took in the view from Etta and Jackson's
house. Allison and I quickly realized the great inspiration many basket weavers draw
from the landscape of this area. The view south of Etta's home slopes gently down
through sagebrush, with the red monuments of the famous valley serving as a back-
drop. A mesa rises to the north of her home and mountains can be viewed in all directions. The sky appears as an expansive blue dome.

We soon realized why Etta delayed meeting us. She reappeared wearing a royal
blue blouse, a blue flowered skirt, with a lime green scarf covering her head. She
looked great! We were escorted to a small shade house where Etta does her basket
work. Split sumac was stacked behind a small camper shell. A small iron cook
stove had pitch heating in a metal basin. Etta had woven two baskets to demonstrate the application of the pitch. Realizing one horsehair handle had loosened, she

Etta's "special red-gold" bag-o-pitch—pinon pitch   Etta's split sumac.
balls Etta gathers on Douglas Mesa.

fixed it before proceeding with the demonstration. Etta always weaves a nicely stitched, well balanced jar. Pitch baskets are not typically woven as finely as coil baskets. Since they are to be sealed with pitch, it is not necessary to have the close stitching required of coil baskets.

Etta produced a small plastic bag filled with balls of pinon pitch. The mesa behind her house is covered with pinon trees. Most contemporary pitch baskets have a golden hue to the pitch. Etta's baskets have a distinctly reddish hue. She searches for pitch that will produce this deep red-gold color, a particular signature of her work. When she was first making baskets, she used to cover the basket with red mud before applying the pitch but has not used this particular method in many years.

Etta explained that she cooks the pitch to a particular consistency. If it is too hot, it becomes runny and will leak through the stitches of the basket. Taking the first basket, she rolled the basket in the hot mixture. It cooled quickly and she was able to grasp the bottom of the basket and proceeded to cover the neck of the jar with pitch. Using a piece of cardboard as a brush, she picked up the hot pitch and brushed it up the neck of the vase. She does not dip the top as she does not wish to get pitch on the horsehair handles. Setting the first basket down, she repeated this procedure with the second basket. By the time she finished the second basket, the first one was ready to be sealed on the inside. Pouring the pitch into the basket, she turned the basket while pouring the excess back into the heated pan. A nearby pan of water was poured into the basket. Etta then let the basket sit for a few moments. This method

Woven baskets before pitch is applied.

serves as the perfect solution for evenly distributing and sealing the pitch on the inside of the basket. In other accounts relating pitch basket making, a procedure that consists of placing hot rocks inside the basket and shaking it vigorously is mentioned for spreading and smoothing the pitch inside of the basket. Etta has never seen or used that method.

Pouring the water from the basket, Etta inspected it for any inconsistencies or bubbles. Spotting an imperfection, Etta held the basket in the cookstove fire, softening the pitch so she was able to push it with her fingers until she was satisfied with the finish. Her baskets bear indelible marks of the handmade process; gentle impressions of her fingerprints can often be spotted on finished baskets. This entire process flows with the seemingly effortless symmetry of one who has practiced her craft for many decades. Throughout the demonstration, Etta was smiling and talking, confident of her ability to produce two more beautiful baskets. At one point in the conversation she lifted her skirt slightly to reveal the horrendous scars resulting from a recent accident. A few months previously, Etta had dropped the hot pitch basin, burning herself badly from her waist to her ankle. Alone at the time, Etta quickly rolled in sand and managed to take care of herself for the next few hours until her husband, Jackson, returned.

Etta dips the bottom of the basket into the hot pitch.

Etta uses a strip of cardboard as a brush to apply hot pitch around the horsehair handles.

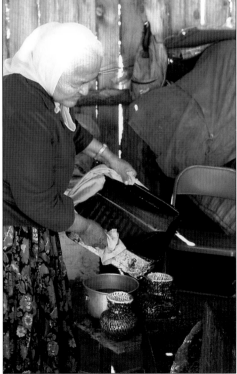

Etta checking the inside of the basket.

Pouring pitch inside the baskets.

Etta seals the pitch inside of the basket by pouring water inside. The equal pressure of the water creates a smooth surface on the inside of the basket.

Etta looks for any imperfections on the exterior surface of the basket. To take out imperfections she softens the pitch by placing the basket in the flames, then smooths the surface with her fingertips. Her fingerprints can be found all over the exterior of the basket, a fitting symbol of the truly handmade nature of the baskets.

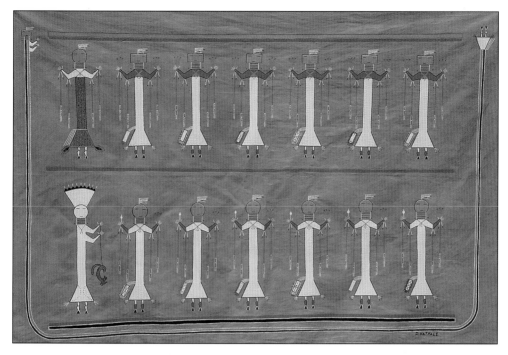

Tó Neinilii appears in the upper left corner in this dry painting of the seventh day of the Na'akai. He is shown at the head of a line of female yé'ii; his shirt spotted with pollen of all colors. Image by Dennis Hathale.

The Nature of Pitch Baskets

Why talk about the pitch baskets (tóshjeeh) in a conversation about Navajo ceremonial baskets? Most writings speak of these baskets, in their everyday role as water carriers or storage baskets which indeed was one of their reasons to exist in the days before metal containers. In looking at the texts of recorded ceremonies, subtle reminders of their use in sacred settings emerges. Reaching far back into the stories of the gods, Tó Neinilii, the Water Sprinkler, is the one to carry the water jug and even today appears with it at his side. He gave the pitch pot to the Navajo people. He is the god of celestial or precipitated waters. When Tó Neinilii wishes to produce rain, he scatters his sacred waters to the four cardinal directions. He also serves as a water carrier for the other gods. He is represented as carrying a wicker water bottle, or two water bottles, one black and one blue. The strings of the divine bottles were rainbows. While Washington Matthews states that during an actual ceremony Tó Neinilii does not appear with a pitch basket at his side, according to several eyewitnesses attending contemporary ceremonies, he does indeed carry one or two at his side. In fact, Tó Neinilii possesses a total of four water bottles—one gold or silver colored, one black, one white, and one blue.

Tó Neinilii appears in the ordinary dress of the male yé'ii, but his accouterments are of inferior quality. His personage is similar to the clown that appears with the Apache crown dancers as well as the Mudheads of the Zuni and Koshares of the Rio Grande Pueblos. Clowning serves a sacred purpose for all of these groups. Through the use of humor, the clown produces laughter, a reaction that helps open an individual and make them more receptive to the healing that must follow. As they say, "Laughter is the best medicine." Washington Matthews made some wonderful observations as to the type of trouble Tó Neinilii is likely to cause.

> While the others are dancing he performs various acts according to his caprice, such as these: He walks along the line of dancers and gets in their way. He dances out of order and out of time. He peers foolishly at different persons. He sits on the ground, his hands clasped across his knees, and rocks his body to and fro. He joins regularly in the dance toward the close of a figure and when the others have retired he remains going through his steps, pretending to be oblivious of their departure; then, feigning to discover their absence, he follows them on a full run. He carries a fox-skin; drops it on the ground; walks away as if unconscious of his loss; pretends to become aware of his loss; acts as if searching anxiously for the skin, which lies in plain sight; screens his eyes with his hand and crouches low to look; imitates in various exaggerated ways the acts of Indian hunters; pretends at length, to find the lost skin; jumps on it as if it were a live animal he was killing; shoulders it and carries it off as if it were a heavy burden; staggers and falls under it. Sometimes he imitates [and mocks] the acts of [Talking God]. (Matthews 1995, 151)

It would be easy to dismiss the Water Sprinkler as a lesser deity if not for the simple fact that he controls the heavenly waters, the most important factor in the continuation of life in the parched landscape of the desert southwest. (A different god is responsible for bodies of water such as oceans, lakes, and rivers.) He is often referenced in the singular, although one is believed to reside at each dwelling place of the yé'ii. When he wishes it to rain, sacred waters are sprinkled in the four directions encouraging storm clouds to come together and produce the moisture. When he desires to produce rain, he scatters his sacred waters to the four cardinal points and immediately the storm clouds begin to gather. We certainly are in need of his services given the droughts this country has suffered in the last few years. Tó Neinilii also appears in the story of the origin of ceremony when The Visionary (Biɫ áhát'íinii) was journeying to the home of the gods in order to learn their medicine ways.

> Now the Thunder People began to make signals. Again and again flashes of lightning descended into the river and a rainbow (nááts'íílid) appeared with its end sticking in one place out of the water. The holy ones in Tse'gi'hi (Tséyi) beheld these signs and thought they must have some meaning for them, so they sent for To'nenili (Tó Neinilii) to find out what they signified. Bearing his two magic water jars, he went to the river where the lightning was flashing and where the rainbow rose. He struck the water to the right with his black jar and to the left with his blue jar, uttering with each motion his peculiar call. As he did this the water opened before him; he descended to the bottom of the stream and found the log. "Who is there?" cried Water Sprinkler. "It is I, Bitahatini (Biɫ áhát'íinii) [The Visionary]," said the voice. (Matthews 1995, 175)

Tapaha (Tábąąhi)—Edge of the Water Clan

The beginning and growth of one of the Navajo clans, Tapaha (Tábąąhi), centers around the pitch water bottle.

> It happened about this time while some of the Tapaha (Tábąąhi) were sojourning at Agathla (Aghaałá), that they sent two children one night to a spring to get water. The children carried out with them two wicker bottles . . . but returned with four. "Where did you get those other bottles?" the parents inquired. "We took them away from two little girls whom we met at the spring," answered the children. "Why did you do this and who are the girls?" asked the elders. "We do not know. They are strangers," said the little ones. The parents at once set out for the spring to find the strange children and restore the stolen bottles to them; but on the way they met the little girls coming toward the Tapaha camp, and asked them who they were. The strange children replied: "We belong to a band of wanderers who are encamped on yonder mountain. They sent us two together to find water." "Then we shall give you a name," said the Tapaha; "We shall call you To'basnaazi (Tó baazhní'ázhí)—Two Come Together For Water." The Tapaha brought the little girls to their hut and bade them be seated. "Stay with us," they said. "You are too weak and little to carry the water so far. We shall send some of our young men to carry it for you." When the young

Gourd cup, probably from Pueblita Canyon Navajo Archaeological Site, circa 1735.

men found the camp of the strangers they invited the latter to visit them. The Tapaha welcomed the newcomers as friends and told them they had already a name for them, Tob'aznaazi. Under this name they became united to the Navajos as a new gens, and they are now closely affiliated with Tapaha. (James 1909, 27-28)

Tó Neinilii, Mixed Water, Sacred Water

Tó Neinilii serves as a water carrier for the other gods. His magical pitch baskets carry the sacred waters needed for ceremonies. This sacred water used to consist of four different types of water: spring or stream water from the east; hail water from the south; rain water from the west; and snow water from the north. (Matthews 1995, 46) Today, the medicine man recreates this mixture as best he can. Medicine men John Holiday and June Blackhorse confirmed that the water is sacred and protected inside the water jug when used in a ceremonial setting. They feel that the pitch basket (tóshjeeh) is the proper receptacle for water along with gourd cups. However, in recent years it is not uncommon for other types of vessels to be used. This special water is used throughout the ceremonies in the preparation of medicines; cigarettes; paint; mixing with yucca root for the ceremonial bath; preparation of sacred mush; in effect, in any ceremony where water is needed. It is not, however, used in the creation of the variety of foods prepared for the fourth night of the nine-day ceremonies.

The sacred water also can be used to bless masks and other sacred objects during a ceremony. Below is a description of the blessing of sacred masks.

> In the meantime the shaman makes, in a water-tight basket, the cold infusion of tsoltsin (tólástsiin). He takes sacred water from a wicker bottle and pours it into the basket in five gourd cupfuls, saving each cupful from a different direction toward the basket; on the surface of the water he may sprinkle dah ts'os, thus forming what is called dah ts'os ke'tlo (kétłoh). At the proper time as indicated by the songs, he bids the boy and girl approach and instructs them in their duties. To the former he gives a black

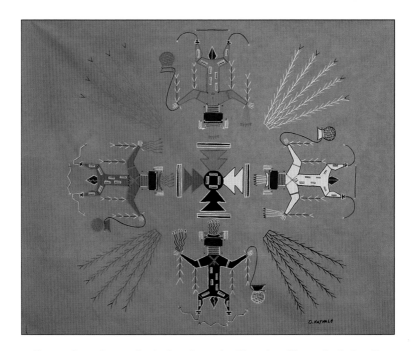

Recreation of a sandpainting from the Shooting Chant depicting Four Water Oxen holding sacred pitch baskets. This painting is used after too much rain.
—Memory aid by Dennis Hathale.
—Courtesy of Georgiana Kennedy Simpson Private Collection.

plumed wand, or india', in each hand; to the other he gives a blue plumed wand in each hand. These wands are taken from a basket at the south-western extremity of the row of masks, etc. The boy, dipping his right-hand wand into the solution, sprinkles the masks and other sacred objects, each row separately, from right to left, the nearer row first. He steps aside and gives way to the girl, who sprinkles exactly in the same manner, from one hand to another, dips and sprinkles as before with the right hand, but with a different wand. Thus the boy and girl continue alternately to dip the wands and sprinkle the sacred objects until each has sprinkled four times. The masks, etc., having been properly asperged, the boy sprinkles the spectators in the north half of the lodge; the girl those in the south half. They sprinkle themselves. The boy sprinkles the bottom of the lodge in the north; the girl does the same in the south. Lastly they sprinkle the roof of the lodge continuing until the infusion is exhausted. They return their wands to the chanter and resume their seats. (Matthews 1902, 107-108)

While not providing the same powerful visual metaphor as the ceremonial bas-ket (t'saa'), the pitch basket is a fixture in Navajo ceremonial settings, playing a more subtle, humble, yet ultimately important role.

8. Ceremonial Basket Etiquette and Safekeeping

It all came to a head one day when I was dealing with a young weaver, spinning her basket, and causing great frustration. There just happened to be another Navajo woman in the store who was paying a great deal of attention to what was happening. The woman's name was Mary Grisham. I knew her well; she had a really bad attitude and was vocal about things that ticked her off; a true radical. As I wrapped up the basket purchase, Mary angrily approached me and said, "Just what do you think you're doing?" Remember, now, that I was very young. At that point I had not learned to deal with angry, aggressive women. I stammered, "What do you mean?" Mary proceeded to inform me that a Navajo basket represents the world; by spinning it the way I did, I caused serious problems. Mary and the weaver stormed out of the trading post, loudly proclaiming my ignorance. I was flabbergasted; I had no idea. I began to ask questions and found books that better explained the meaning behind the baskets. I found that the traditional basket was a sacred object, used by medicine men to practice healing ceremonies. The interpretation of the weaving is deep and meaningful; much reverence goes into its creation. This was to say nothing of the pictorial baskets that I had carelessly spun that were depictions of Chant Ways, morality tales, and legendary heroes. My basket spinning had caused such a disturbance because it showed disrespect. In effect, it had caused a chaotic reaction in a spiritual sense. Not good, I assure you. I was then, and still am, embarrassed by my lack of compassion and understanding. It was a hard lesson, but one I have learned well. I have also gained a great deal of humility and now work hard to recognize what the weavers are trying to say through their art.

Barry Simpson

Navajo basket artist Evelyn Cly with two of her children, seventeen year-old daughter, Martina, and her twelve year-old son, Theodore.

Ceremonial baskets are one of the most treasured items in Navajo households. They are important for use in ceremonies and as a sacred storage area for heirlooms such as family jewelry, making the basket an important part of a traditional home. Certain rules apply to the proper storage and display of ceremonial baskets within the home. These rules demonstrate the concept of the basket as an entity possessing its own spirit.

Master basket artist, Evelyn Cly had these comments: "You don't hang it on the wall with a nail. How would you like a nail in you?!"

I asked how she hung the baskets in her own home. "I make a thread loop," she answered, "and hang it with the loop."

We had a lively conversation with four members of the Beginning Navajo Culture class at Monument Valley High School in Kayenta, Arizona. These particular students chose to weave baskets during the 2001 spring term. Their teacher, Sara Stanley, required each student to finish two baskets during the term.

New weavers at Monument Valley High School Beginning Navajo Culture Class, Kayenta, Navajo Nation. Students clockwise from left: Abraham Black, J.D. Kinlacheeny, Tee Jai James, and Crystal Black.

Beyond learning the technical aspects of basket making, it soon became apparent that the story of the basket and its proper care were every bit as important to these students as the weaving itself.

"You can use it for decoration, but not on the wall because you pour out the goodness or medicine. You don't poke a hole in the center because it is like poking a hole in your mind or abrupting the start of your life."

Imagine a Navajo person's consternation upon walking into many of the old time trading posts and seeing baskets nailed to the walls and ceilings of the store! It is important to note here that this particular display technique by traders, beginning with early Navajo reservation entrepreneurs such as Lorenzo Hubbell, comes from their deep, personal affection for Navajo ceremonial baskets.

Ceremonial baskets on the ceiling of Turney's Trading Post in Gallup, New Mexico.

These traditional concepts voiced by weavers and students may put many basket collectors in a quandary as to the proper display of the basket in your home. Before running for the hammer to pull baskets off of the wall, consider these thoughts. Most Navajo people delineate between a basket that is serving a purpose in their own home versus the basket as an art object. Many Navajo people hang baskets on the wall for safekeeping as well as for their enjoyment.

A great explanation of this separation of purposes can be found in the fine book *Molded in the Image of Changing Woman* by Maureen Trudelle Schwartz. In a conversation the author had with Avery Dennis of Tsaile, Arizona, he was asked what would happen to a basket if it were sold to someone living off the reservation. Avery Dennis answered, "There is no life to it, it is just a design. But once it [the basket] goes back into the four sacred mountains . . . it comes back to life. Or, if it was brought back to that woman that wove it, and then that automatically, that spirit is going to go back into it. It would recognize [her, the weaver]."

Maureen Schwartz pressed further, "What if it was used in a ceremony? But not by the woman that wove it. Would it become alive during the ceremony?"

"Yes. It would be. But once it leaves the ceremony if it was for a patient, and then that [patient] she would have belief that this is a sacred thing, but then it will, her, the way that she [the weaver] understands this pattern that she did, it will help the patient to heal, too. And then when the medicine man gets it, when the medicine man gets it, it will separate. Just like the weaving part will go back to the lady [the weaver], and then the healing part will go to the patient, but then when it gets into the medicine man, her or his belief is going to go in there. Then it is his [the medicine man's]. That is how it works. But then if he [the medicine man] takes it to Gallup to sell it, it [the inner being] comes back to him. This is nothing but a basket, but if somebody else buys it again for a ceremonial purpose, for a reason, for a purpose, when it gets into that ceremonial hooghan, that spirit is going to go back in there again. . . . It works like that." Avery chuckled.

Many families have baskets that have been passed down for generations. I visited Darlene Eddie, a resident of the Utah strip of the Navajo nation. Darlene has been charged as the person in this generation with the safekeeping of the Gladys Yellowman family basket. This basket has been passed down from her maternal great-grandmother and is currently being used by four generations of the family for a variety of ceremonies. It was most recently used during a Kinaaldá, the Navajo girl's coming of age ceremony. Darlene's sister, Molly Yellowman, recounted how this basket has been used for every family ceremony she can remember. They now

Private Navajo ceremonial basket collection of trader Russell Griswold.

cover the basket in plastic wrap before placing any meal or other items in the basket, since it is so old that they wish to take the best possible care of it.

For decades, many Navajo people including medicine practitioners have used another method for storing their valuables—the local trader or pawnbroker. Far from being a relic of the past, pawning ceremonial baskets remains one of the best ways to store baskets. Typically a person can expect to receive a loan of ten to twenty dollars for the basket. He then makes regular payments to the pawn broker, which may include part of the original loan plus interest. This method has proven to be a very inexpensive way to keep baskets in a safe place until they are needed for the next ceremony. This service is especially valuable in areas where no basket making takes place.

Russell Griswold has been running an active pawn business in Tse Bonito, New Mexico, for twenty-five years. His personal interest in baskets can be seen in his extensive private collection of Navajo baskets. When I asked Russell why he chooses to collect the baskets, he replied, "How can you begin to replace these baskets? They are just too hard to make!"

At the time of our conversation Russell had 1,509 baskets in active pawn. I wondered, "What percentage are pawned for safekeeping versus strictly for money?"

"Oh, I would say, ninety-eight to ninety-nine percent of the baskets we get are strictly for safekeeping. We probably see ten baskets a week from medicine men."

"How many baskets will end up dead pawn?" (Dead pawn means the person did not repay their loan within the designated time. After a prescribed waiting period, the basket becomes available for resale.)

Russell replied, "In the last pull, probably only about twenty baskets. One thing . . . I don't wholesale these baskets to other dealers. I keep them to sell

Navajo ceremonial baskets in pawn at Griswolds.

to the Navajo people for their use. I currently have about two hundred in the vault. They'll all be gone by June."

9. Teaching Navajo Culture to Future Generations

Due to their great concern over the loss of Navajo culture and identity in the younger generations, Robert and Ruth Roessel founded the Rough Rock Demonstration School in 1966.

"It was the wisdom of the School Board that saw the danger of allowing two traditional Navajo crafts to die out that gave rise to the Navajo arts and crafts community training program. It brought adults throughout the reservation to Rough Rock to learn these traditional crafts." (Robert Roessel 1983:IX)

The example set by the Rough Rock Demonstration School has been followed by other communities through the formation of Navajo cultural programs in schools on and off the reservation. One of the many challenges in developing such programs is finding qualified instructors, those who are not only good teachers but also have an extensive knowledge of the culture. Sara Stanley, the Navajo culture instructor at Monument Valley High School in Kayenta, Arizona, embodies these traits. Finding Sara was a bit of an event. I learned about her program through a young basket weaver, Martina Cly, who brings her work to the trading post. She spoke about classes available at her high school. I began by leaving messages for Sara. Additionally, Allison Billy began looking for her during his weekends spent in Kayenta. Sara was

Sara Stanley, Navajo culture instructor in Kayenta, Arizona, demonstrating sumac splitting.

curious about the two people out looking for her but soon realized that we came with good intentions.

Sara has been teaching at the high school for the past three years and one can say she comes by her talents genetically. Her mother, Emma Becenti, instructed the same courses at the high school for twenty-five years preceding Sara's tenure. When Emma was considering retirement, she contacted Sara, who was living in Phoenix at the time, and told Sara that she needed to think about taking over the program. Sara held off until she was able to get her son and older daughter graduated from high school and headed off to college. She felt her younger daughter, in second grade at the time, could make the transition from Phoenix to Kayenta.

Sara learned to make baskets when she was in high school. Her father did not make much money and she wanted to help. Her mother knew a little about making baskets, so Sara and her mother proceeded to learn side by side, going to Sara's three aunts, Jessie Holiday, Lilly Phillips, and Rose Begay, to learn more about making baskets. Sara was frustrated by the difficult process of finding and preparing materials. She and Emma would typically go near Farmington, New Mexico, over an hour's drive, to find the sumac. Sumac (chiiłchin) is a tough, woody plant, so she was cut and scraped during the gathering process. Emma made it clear from the beginning that Sara was to learn the correct way. After they learned to make the baskets, Emma would go to area trading posts to sell them. Later, Navajo people came to them to buy baskets for ceremonies. While Emma's first love is beadwork (particularly fine hatbands), she still makes baskets to order.

After speaking with Sara, Allison Billy and I met six students from her beginning and advanced classes. Sara teaches rug weaving, sash weaving, beadwork, and basket making. At the beginning of each semester, the students choose which art form they wish to learn. These classes are not simply craft classes. Navajo artwork is intricately tied with the story of the Navajo people. Through the artwork, Sara is able to tell the stories of how the Navajo people came to be, where the art forms originated, and the beliefs integral to being Navajo. The students ranged in

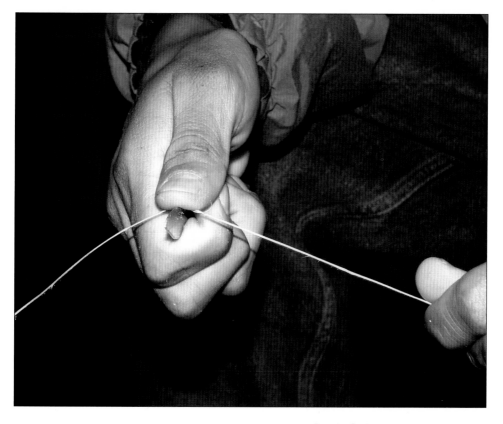

Dustin Sullivan trimming a splint.

age from fourteen to seventeen years old and were evenly split between male and female. I asked seventeen year old Dustin Sullivan why he chose to make baskets.

"I had taken a class from Sara before." Dustin answered. "I watched her make the baskets and wanted to learn. I wanted to help other Navajo people by making something for healing." He reflected for a moment. "It takes patience. Making it is easy—to make it good is hard. The start and finish are the hardest. To make the start, keeping it round and keeping the sumac from breaking, is hard. The finish is hard because it takes more time."

Freda Cook, a junior at Monument Valley High School, took the class from Sara during her freshman year and decided to take the advanced class this year. Freda spoke of her motivation. "I had tried all of the other art forms. No one is making baskets in my family, so I wanted to try it." There were some surprises. "It takes too long. When I started, it was very hard. My hands were very sore and tired."

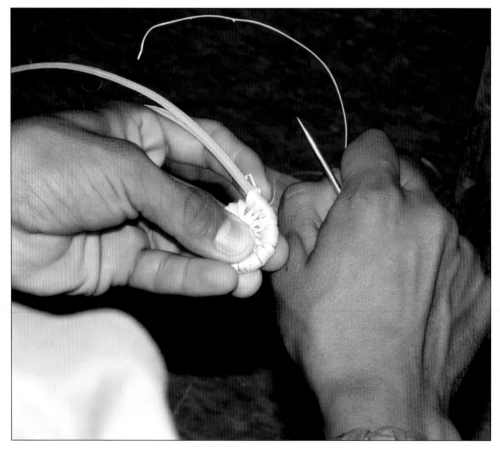

"To make the start, keeping it round and keeping the sumac from breaking, is hard."
—Dustin Sullivan

Freda Cook, Monument Valley High School student.

I asked Freda if she had seen the basket used in a traditional ceremony.

"Yes," she smiled, "in my sister's traditional wedding in July, 1999. They had corn mush in the basket, filled to the red part. They ate out of the basket. They had a pitch water jug and washed their hands with the water."

The next group consisted of a lively foursome in Sara's beginning class. I knew things would get interesting the moment fifteen-year old Abraham Black walked in. His face brightened, and he came forward immediately to discover what was going on. The room layout has a display case of students' handiwork as you first enter the room. Tables are set up in the front for instruction and students working on beading. Behind the tables are the rug and sash looms. Finally, in the back corner is a round table with a stack of reeds on the shelf. They use reeds instead of sumac for the class since reeds are easier to obtain and moisten faster than sumac.

Tee Jai James tying a splint.

Tee Jai James, at sixteen the oldest, talked about why she turned to baskets. "I wanted to try . . . my grandmother, Bertha Simpson, is a medicine woman, an herbalist."

Crystal Begay, fourteen, also draws on her roots. "I wanted to learn because of my great-grandma. Basket weaving has been in my family for a long time. I'm working on my second basket in class, but I've also learned it from my grandma, Edith Denetsosie."

"I just chose it," spoke up another student, fourteen-year old J.D. Kinlacheeny, "Just to do it. My family never did baskets."

The students went about their work. Finally I asked Abraham, "Why are you biting the basket? It looks like you are eating the basket."

"If it goes like a bowl, I need to bite on it so to straighten it out. My grandma, Margie Parrish, taught me."

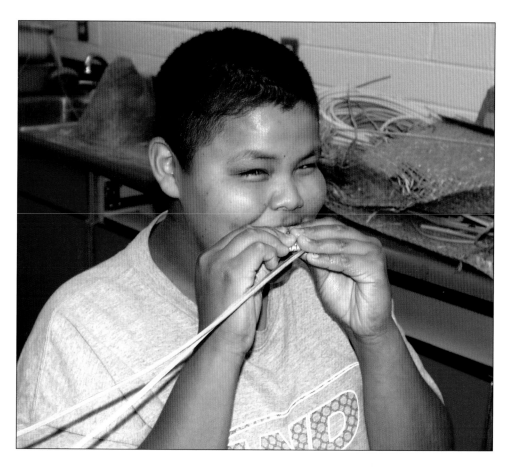

Abraham Black bites the basket in order to keep it straight.

The students wanted me to understand the proper conduct in regard to the basket. "You don't put it on your head. It will stunt your growth. Don't spin it as that will mix up your thoughts and shorten your memory."

Crystal was emphatic, "You don't want to throw it around or burn it."

"Why not?" I asked.

Everyone joined in, "It's like throwing yourself around. It's a matter of self-respect. Burning the basket is like an offense to Mother Earth. You can't burn the sumac because it comes from Mother Earth."

The students agreed that J.D. was the fastest basket maker. "He can finish in a couple of hours. It takes the rest of us up to three hours."

J.D. explained his speed. "When you finish the basket, you have to finish it in one day or you will go blind."

After meeting with these students I felt more hope for the preservation of Navajo culture among the young people. Many of the students have plans to go to

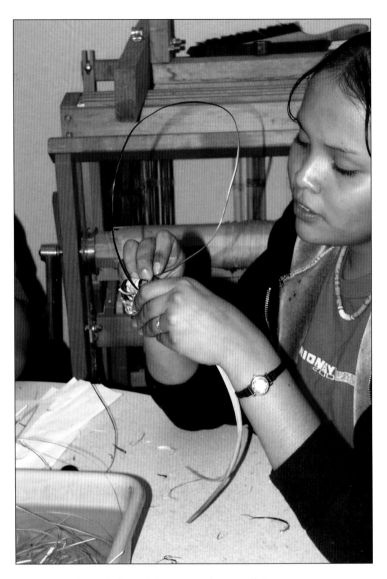

Beginning student, Crystal Begay, sewing a splint.

college. While only half the students expressed a desire to continue basket making, all of them demonstrated great pride in who they are as individuals and as
members of the Navajo Nation. I believe Sara, through her teaching, is one of the
reasons behind their sense of pride and place. She feels strongly that people who
have knowledge need to pass it on. I have found this to be a particular sticking point
across the generations according to Navajo people with whom I have spoken.
Medicine men are anxious for the information to be passed on rather than die with
them. They, along with other elders, point out that they have a wealth of information

and experience, but no one is asking them to share it. Some elders feel that the younger generations have no respect for them. Traditionally, when you approach someone and ask them to share their knowledge, you must be ready to offer some type of payment for their wealth of experience. Younger people feel this knowledge should be freely given. An additional factor in the breakdown of cross-generational relationships is a language barrier that has sprung up.

Clayton Long is the bilingual coordinator for the San Juan School District in southeastern Utah. The southern portion of this very large district is predominantly Navajo. He points out that in the latest assessment of Navajo language taken in 2000, there are no children below fourth grade level in the entire county that are literate in Navajo. The elder population in this same area have limited or no proficiency in the English language. The task of providing cultural training for the younger generations has become overwhelming. Thankfully, teachers like Sara, medicine men like John and June, and administrators like Clayton, all are willing to share their information and work diligently against the tide of Navajo cultural loss.

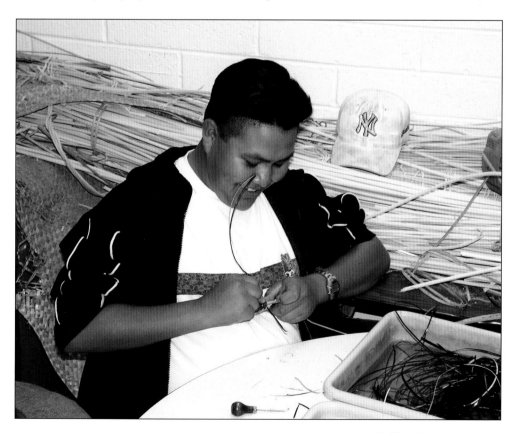

J. D. Kinlacheeny weaving.

10. Honoring the Weavers

Perhaps no other cluster of cultural traits more clearly reveals the Navajo value on beauty than do their various arts and crafts. Beauty and harmony are two cornerstones of Navajo life, and both find their clear expression in the separate as well as collective arts and crafts. The Navajos never were a people who believed it was necessary to possess the tangible evidence of beauty or harmony, but they were a people who believed that even the mundane and everyday world could be and should be beautiful. (Robert A. Roessel, Jr, Rough Rock Demonstration School, Roessel 1983:VIII)

Navajo ceremonial baskets are in the rather unique position of being a sacred item with a commercial market. Charlotte Frisbie points out, "The only ceremonial objects regularly seen today besides commercial sandpaintings are "wedding baskets," which are required in many ceremonies" (Frisbie 1987, 132-133). Susan Brown McGreevy makes the same observation in her 1993 *Messenger* article, "The other weavers: Navajo basket makers and the Museum's collection." She states, "It seems probable that economic incentives were responsible for a gradual relaxation of traditional Navajo taboos relating to production of the t'aa' (ts'aa'). Basket making was no longer considered solely within a ritual context, but came to be viewed as a viable source of personal and family income." This point is driven home by

Contemporary Rain Cross basket by Peggy Black—1997.
—Courtesy Simpson Family Collection.

Navajo basketmaker, Peggy Black. She started weaving baskets because she need-
ed money for school supplies. Her mom and dad didn't go to school so they didn't
have a lot of money. She sold her first basket to Bob Hosler at Thin Bear Trading
Post because that is where her mother, Grace Rock, sold her baskets. She used to
sell baskets to "Chin" Smith at Oljato, Gouldings, and Lee Trading in Kayenta.
Peggy's daughters, Raelynn and Sonja, got into basket making for the same reason.
Peggy's sister, Evelyn Cly, started weaving pitch pots when she was six years old.
She made the regular ceremonial basket when she was eight years old. She was
taught by her paternal grandmother, Wanda Rock. Her grandmother made the pitch
pots. Her mother, Grace Rock, did the regular baskets. Evelyn was raised by her
grandmother, Wanda. Her grandmother would sell her baskets for her. She was

Evelyn Cly weaving "The People Ceremonial."
—Courtesy Simpson Family Private Collection.

eleven or twelve years old when she started doing her own selling to the Hunts at San Juan Trading in Mexican Hat, Utah. Evelyn started weaving to help bring in money for the family. Today, she can weave a fifteen-inch basket in two and a half days if she works on it for seven hours each day.

Foutz irregular basket.—Courtesy John and Jacque Foutz Collection.

Hubble irregular basket.—Courtesy Hubble Trading Post National Historical Monument, Ganado, Arizona.

Separation of the Navajo and Hopi People Basket by Peggy Black.
—Courtesy of Simpson Family Collection.

Two baskets captured my imagination more than any others. John and Jacque Foutz possess the first one; the other hangs on the ceiling inside Hubbell Trading Post. For most people, these two baskets, if up for a vote, would have been selected "Least Likely to Capture Anyone's Imagination." So, why am I fascinated? In the scheme of Navajo art, in fact, the Navajo point of view, these two weavings do not fit in. Many people have documented the Navajo drive toward balance and harmony. If one looks at these two baskets, you notice that the coils are beautifully woven. The design elements, however, are random, crooked, and unbalanced. I spotted the first basket in the Foutz collection and found it interesting, but upon seeing the second basket, obviously woven by the same woman, a weaver who lived over a century ago, I couldn't

One of the largest ceremonial baskets ever created—32½" diameter.
—Woven by Mary and her daughter, Sally Black in the late 1970s.
Shown here are Mary Holiday Black, her granddaughter, Kayla, and my son, Grange.
—Courtesy of the Simpson Family Collection.

Basket depicting the placing of the stars by First Man and Coyote.
—Woven by Lorraine Black in1996.
—Courtesy Simpson Family Collection.

help but wonder what motivated her to create technically beautiful weavings with such a strange interpretation of design? We will never know the answer to that question, yet these baskets, more than any others I viewed, represent the difference between "just a design" and individual expression.

We are currently in a dynamic renaissance of Navajo basket weaving predominantly led by a group of weavers from the Douglas Mesa area of the Navajo reservation. Variations in Navajo basket designs were virtually nonexistent throughout the middle decades of the 1900s. Starting around 1970, experiments with form and design started to appear. Leading the way is famed basket maker, Mary Holiday Black, recipient of a National Endowment of the Humanities Fellowship, the first Navajo and first Utahan ever to be so honored. Mary learned to weave baskets at the age of eleven from her grandmother's relatives. Now, for over half a century, she has not only been

Basket by Joann Johnson.
—Courtesy Twin Rocks Trading Post.

weaving baskets that redefine the concept of Navajo basketry, but as the matriarch of a family of eleven children, nine of whom are weavers, and now with countless grandchildren, many who have taken up the weaving mantel, Mary is the quiet force behind this movement. Mary expresses her personal philosophy regarding the baskets, "Each ceremonial basket has a story. There are many basket stories. If we stop making the baskets, we lose the stories."

The floodgates have since opened producing a range of designs never before seen in any variety of Native American basketry. It produces an interesting dilemma as many of these variants are considered taboo by the majority of Navajo people. Evelyn Cly follows this belief. She has, however, created some ceremonial baskets with three-dimensional woven figures, something she feels does not go too far astray. Not only are weavers creating new variations, but some of the designs that harken back a century before are finding a new life under the guidance of the weaver's fingers.

Some weavers also believe that by weaving the special Chantway designs, they are helping preserve their traditional stories and, therefore, a part of their heritage. I know many of the new designs have opened a channel for discussion between younger weavers who previously did not have any background in their origin stories and the older people regarding the meaning of particular designs. When Mary Black's daughter, Lorraine, was interpreting for Mary, instead of it simply being a time of information gathering for this book, the dynamics of the conversation evolved into Mary having an opportunity to teach Lorraine in traditional ways and Lorraine being open to the lessons provided by her mother.

Other basketmakers are pursuing new design variations as an expression of their own personal artistic abilities. One of the most dynamic of these contemporary weavers is Joann Johnson. A fourth generation Navajo basket weaver, she has a passionate awareness of her heritage and history. Born and raised in Monument Valley, she has spent her life in the Navajo heartland, surrounded by the sacred mountains and monuments that tell the stories of her people's past. Joann feels a responsibility to help preserve that past by preserving her culture. Basket weaving is one way she demonstrates her commitment to her convictions. "It's a gift," she says of her weaving abilities, "I learned it from my mother, who learned from her mother, who learned from her mother, my great-grandmother Ida Bigman. I feel close to her when I am weaving a basket." More than any other weaver, she takes the concept

Basket woven honoring the millennium by Sally Black. —Courtesy Simpson Family Collection.

Ad for foreign made baskets with a ceremonial design in their midst.

Late 1800s cloud design basket.—Courtesy John and Jacque Foutz Collection.

Modern cloud design basket. —Courtesy Twin Rocks Trading Post.

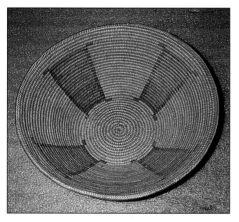

Late 1800s four blankets basket. —Courtesy Museum of Indian Art & Culture.

Karen Kearn holding Cora Black's three blankets basket.

of colors that are a part of every day, and combines them into representations of the changes in sunlight throughout the day. Joann says the money she gets from selling her baskets is not a driving force for her. "It's not the money as much as it is the accomplishment," she asserts. She enjoys creating beautiful things, taking the ideas that come to her and making them real, bringing them to fruition. This may be one of the reasons her baskets are so beautiful, because she has such a love for her art.

In viewing the progression of baskets through time, they have seen many revolutions that began long ago in Ancestral Puebloans baskets and moved forward into contemporary baskets. The designs have ebbed and flowed depending on the dynam-

This basket by Mary Black, showing the Fire Dance, launched contemporary weavings depicting Chantway and other story baskets. —Courtesy Simpson Family Private Collection.

This modern basket with three rectangles and three rain cross designs relates back to basket designs from the late 1800s.—Courtesy Simpson Family Private Collection.

Ceremonial baskets come full circle. Artist Lorraine Black depicts the Night Chant ceremony in two baskets: one showing the dancers outside of the hooghan and upon lifting the basket, the ceremony within the hooghan is revealed.—Courtesy of Twin Rocks Trading Post.

ics and constraints of the time. I cannot help but feel that Navajo baskets have evolved into a reflection of themselves and the Navajo people, which means that they are exactly the same. The Navajo ceremonial basket has led to baskets depicting ceremony. We've reached the end of the book, but not the end of the story. I hope this book will provoke discussion about the basket, bringing forth other stories while opening up more opportunities for learning the story about the basket—about the People—about life.

Glossary

Aghaałá—(Agathla) "much wool area" is the literal translation. Aghaałá is the
    name of a prominent volcanic plug in Monument Valley

Áłtsé Hooghan—House God

Anaa' jí ndáá'—The Enemy Way Ceremony

Asdzáá Nádleehé—Changing Woman, grows old and young at will. From her union
with Jóhonaa'éí, the Bearer of the Sun, was born the Hero Twins.

atiin—road, pathway

azee' dah'ats'os—medicine that comes to a point; hoarfrost medicine

Beehoochidii—the Great God

Bigháá' ask'idii—"Bearer of seed to men." The humpback yé'ii

Bił áhát'íinii—The Visionary, Bił = with him, hát'íinii = envisioning

chiiłchin—Sumac, *Rhus trilobata*, the plant material used for making baskets.

ch'ó—(Tchoh-ranh) evergreen tree

dah ts'os—hoarfrost

Diné—The Navajo People

Dinétah—among the Navajo, Dinétah is the name of the original dwelling place of
    the Navajo People southeast of Bloomfield, New Mexico.

Diyin Dine'é—Holy People

diyinii—holy; the one that is holy

Dontso—Big Fly

Dziłk'ihjí—Mountain Top Way, Dziłk'ihjí, is one of the nine day ceremonies.

Haashch'ééłchíí'—Red Talking God

Hashch'ééłti'í—Talking God

hataałii—singer, a medicine man

Hochxó'í—evil

Hóchxǫ'íjí—The Evil Way Ceremony

hooghan—a traditional Navajo home

Hózhǫ́ǫ́jí—Blessingway Ceremony

Huerfano—Spanish name for one of the sacred mesas

'iiná—life, living according to the Navajo way

jaatł'óół—(Jacla) jaa = ear, tł'óół = string—Heishi loops of stone, typically turquoise,
    worn as earrings, most often looped on a heishi necklace. Traditional earrings
    which are typically tied to the bottom of a turquoise necklace.

jish—medicine bundle or bundles

Jóhonaa'éí—the bearer of the sun and father of the Hero Twins

k'eet'áán—prayerstick

kétłoh—ké = feet + tłoh = application—Medicine which is both imbibed by the
    patient, and placed on the patient's body. The feet and legs are the starting
    point. There are many kinds of kétłoh, each corresponding to a different
    ceremonial. For example: Tł'ééjí kétłoh = Night Chant infusion, Chíshíjí
    kétłoh = Chiricahua Way infusion.

Kiis'áanii—Pueblo People—Kin = house, s'á = sits there, nii = noun maker

Kinaaldá—girl's coming-of-age ceremony

Kin łichíi'nii—Clan of The Red House People

Na'akai—another term for the Yé'ii Bicheii

nááts'íílid—rainbow

Naayéé' Neezghání—Monster Slayer, one of the Hero Twins born of Changing Woman

nahagha'—ceremony

nitł'iz—sacred stones and shells

Pai—Pai tribes, in this book, specifically the southern Paiutes.

shá bikétł'óól—sun rays, rainbow spots which show the patient where to kneel and where to put their hands as they drink from a basket during a ceremony. (See image on page 23.)

Tábąąhí—(Tapaha) Edge of the Water Clan.

Tchoh-ranh—(ch'ó) evergreen tree

tł'éé'jí biyiin—(Tsalye' Bigi'n) Darkness songs

Tó baazhní'ázhí—Two Come Together For Water

Tó bájíshchiní—Born-for-Water, one of the Navajo Hero Twins born of Changing Woman

Tó lanastsi'—(Tó ałtaanásdziid) Tó = water + ałtaanásdziid' = mixed or sacred water

tólástsiin—Lotions created for external use during a healing ceremony. Also, the bat used during shoe game.

Tó Neinilii—tó = water + neinilghe = sprinkles it about + ii = the one—The Water Sprinkler, one of the Holy People

tóshjeeh—pitch basket

ts'aa'—Navajo ceremonial basket or baskets

ts'aa' hadoodzaa—(dsahadoldza)—ts'aa' = basket, hadooidzaa = dressed

Tséníchii'—People of the white rock with a red streak through it.

tséyi'—in the canyon

tsihał—(Tsin-tralth)—rock club

tsiiyééł—hair bundle design

yebaka—female yé'ii

yé'ii—Deity or deities

Yé'ii Bicheii—Holy Beings (People) grandfather of the yé'ii, the impersonator of Haashch'éélti'í in the Night Chant, and leader of the yé'ii impersonators/masked dancers. The ceremony is entitled Tł'éé' jí, but commonly referred to as Na'akai or Yé'ii Bicheii.

Yé'ii dine'é—Holy People

yé'iitsoh—(Yeitsoh) Big Yéi, the fiercest of the alien monsters plaguing the Navajo people.

yoołgai ts'aa'—white shell basket

Zaad doolzhaa'í—zaad = word + doolzhaa' = rough + í = noun maker—Fringe Mouth

Zenichi—(Correctly Tséníchii') People of the white rock with a red streak through it.

Sources

Bailey, Garrick and Roberta Glenn Baily, *A History of the Navajos—The Reservation Years*. Santa Fe, New Mexico: School of American Research Press.

Begay, Shirley M. *Kinaalda': A Navajo Puberty Ceremony*. Revised Edition, Rough Rock, Arizona: Rough Rock Demonstration School, 1983.

Brown, Gary M. "Old Wood and Early Navajo: A Chronometric Analysis of the Dinétah Phase." In *Dine' Bikeyah: Papers in Honor of David M. Brugge*. Meliha S. Duran and David T. Kirkpatrick, editors. pp. 39-51, Albuquerque, New Mexico: Archaeological Society of New Mexico: 24, 1998.

Brugge, David M., and Charlotte Frisbie, editors. *Papers in Honor of Leland C. Wyman*. Santa Fe, New Mexico: The Museum of New Mexico Press, 1982.

Brugge, David M. "Navajo Archaeology: A Promising Past." In *The Archaeology of Navajo Origins*. Ronald H. Towner, editor, pp. 255-271. Salt Lake City, Utah: University of Utah Press, 1996.

Brugge, David M. "A History of the Chaco Navajos." In *Reports of the Chaco Center*, W. James Judge, editor. Albuquerque, New Mexico: Division of Chaco research, National Park Service, 1979.

Bunte, Pamela A. "Ethnohistory of the San Juan Paiute Tribe." In *Translating Tradition: Basketry Arts of the San Juan Paiute*, edited by Susan Brown McGreevy and Andrew Hunter Whiteford. Santa Fe: Wheelwright Museum of the American Indian, 1985.

Campbell, Joseph. *The Hero's Adventure, The Power of Myth*. Interview by Bill Moyers, 1996.

Chiao, Chien. "Navajo Sandpainting and Tibetan Mandala: A Preliminary Comparison." *Papers in Honor of Leland C. Wyman*, pp. 21-26, Santa Fe, New Mexico: Museum of New Mexico Press, 1982.

Copeland, James M. "Navajo Hero Twin Ceremonial Art in Dinétah." In *Dine' Bikeyah: Papers in Honor of David M. Brugge*. Meliha S. Duran and David T. Kirkpatrick, editors, pp. 57-66, Albuquerque, New Mexico: Archaeological Society of New Mexico: 24, 1998.

Dunmire, William W., and Gail D. Tierney. *Wild Plants and Native Peoples of the Four Corners*. Santa Fe: Museum of New Mexico Press, 1997.

Dutton, Bertha P. and Caroline B. Olin. "Sandpaintings of Sam Tilden, Navajo Medicine Man." *Papers in Honor of Leland C. Wyman*, pp 58-67, Santa Fe, New Mexico: Museum of New Mexico Press, 1982.

Edison, Carol A. "Willow Stories: An Introduction," In *Willow Stories—Utah Navajo Baskets*, edited by Carol A. Edison. Salt Lake: Utah Arts Council, 1996.

Farella, John R. *The Main Stalk: A Synthesis of Navajo Philosophy*. Tucson: University of Arizona Press, 1984.

Farella, John, "Foreword" In *The Night Chant—A Navajo Ceremony*.Washington Matthews. Originally published; New York: Knickerbocker Press, 1902. Salt Lake City: University of Utah Press, 1995.

Farmer, Malcolm F. "Bear Ceremonialism Among Navajos and Other Apacheans." *Papers in Honor of Leland C. Wyman*, pp. 110-114. Santa Fe, New Mexico: Museum of New Mexico Press, 1982.

Fetterman, Jerry. "Radiocarbon and Tree-Ring Dating at Early Navajo Sites: Examples from the Aztec Area." In *The Archaeology of Navajo Origins*. Ronald H. Towner editor, pp. 71-82. Salt Lake City, Utah: University of Utah Press, 1996.

Fishler, Stanley, *Symbolism of a Navajo "Wedding" Basket.* Masterkey 33(6) Los Angeles: Southwest Museum, 1954.

Franciscan Fathers, The. *An Ethnologic Dictionary of the Navajo Language.* Saint Michaels, Arizona: Navajo Indian Mission, 1910.

Fray Alonso de Benavides. *The Memorial of Fray Alonso de Benavides,* 60, notes.

Frisbie, Charlotte J. *Navajo Medicine Bundles or Jish: Acquisition, Transmission, and Disposition in the Past and Present.* Albuquerque: University of New Mexico Press, 1987.

Frisbie, Charlotte J. "Epilogue In Southwestern Indian Ritual Drama." Charlotte J. Frisbie, editor, pp. 307-343, *School of American Research Advanced Seminar Series*, Albuquerque: University of New Mexico Press, 1980a.

Frisbie, Charlotte J. "Ritual Drama in the Navajo House Blessing Ceremony In Southwestern Indian Ritual Drama." Charlotte J. Frisbie, editor, pp. 161-190, *School of American Research Advanced Seminar Series*, Albuquerque: University of New Mexico Press, 1980b.

Frisbie, Charlotte J. "An Approach to the Ethnography of Navajo Ceremonial Performance." *In the Ethnography of Musical Performance*, Norma Mcleod and Marcia Herndon, editors, pp. 75-104, Norwood, Pennsylvania: Norwood Editions, 1980c.

Frisbie, Charlotte J. "The Navajo House Blessing Ceremonial." *El Palacio* 75 (3): 26-35, 1968.

Frisbie, Charlotte J. "The Navajo House Blessing Ceremonial: A Study of Cultural Change." Ph.d. dissertation, Department of Anthropology, University of New Mexico, Ann Arbor: University Microfilms, 1970.

Frisbie, Charlotte J. *Kinaalda': A Study of the Navajo Girl's Puberty Ceremony.* Middletown, Connecticut: Wesleyan University Press, 1967.

Gill, Sam. *Native American Religious Action: A Performance Approach to Religion,* Columbia, South Carolina: University of South Carolina, 1987.

Gregory, William K. and Milo Hellman. "The Dentition of Dryopithecus and the Origin of Man." *Anthropological Papers of the American Museum of Natural History*, Vol. XXVII, Part 1, New York: The American Museum of Natural History, 1926.

Haile, Berard. "Emergence Myth According to the Hanelthnayhe or Upward Reaching Rite," *Navajo Religion Series*, Vol III, Museum of Navajo Ceremonial Art, Santa Fe, New Mexico: 1949.

Haile, Berard. *Head and Face Masks in Navajo Ceremonialism.* Saint Michaels, Arizona: St. Michael's Press, 1947.

Hester, James J. *Early Navajo Migrations and Acculturation in the Southwest.* Santa Fe: Museum of New Mexico Papers in Anthropology, 1962.

Hill, W.W. "Navaho Trading and Trading and Trading Ritual: A Study in of Cultural Dynamic." *Southwestern Journal of Anthropology* 4(4): 371-396, 1948.

Hill, W.W. "Some Navajo Culture Changes During Two Centuries." In *Essays in Historical Anthropology in Honor of John R. Swanton*, Smithsonian Miscellaneous Collection, no. 100. Washington: Smithsonian Institution.

Hogan, Patrick. "Navajo-Pueblo Interaction During the Gobernador Phase: A Reassessment of the Evidence." *In Rethinking Navajo Pueblitos*. pp. 3-22, Albuquerque, New Mexico: Bureau of Land Management, Cultural Resources Series No. 8, 1991.

James, George Wharton. *Indian Basketry.* New York: Dover Publications, Inc., 1909.

James, George Wharton. *Indian Basketry and How To Make Indian and Other Baskets.* New York, New York: Henry Malkan, 1903.

Janus, S. "Letter to commissioner of Indian Affairs." Los Angeles Federal Archives and Records Center, Record Group 75, Tuba City Superintendent's Letters Sent, Box 6, Vol. 71, January 23, 1909.

Jett, Stephen C. "Territory and Hogan: Local Homelands of the Navajo." In *Dine' Bikeyah: Papers in Honor of David M. Brugge.* Meliha S. Duran and David T. Kirkpatrick, editors, pp. 117-123, Albuquerque, New Mexico: Archaeological Society of New Mexico: 24, 1998.

Kearns, Timothy M. "Protohistoric and Early Historic Navajo Lithic Technology in Northwest New Mexico." In *The Archaeology of Navajo Origins.* Ronald H. Towner editor, pp. 109-145. Salt Lake City, Utah: University of Utah Press, 1996.

Kelley, Klara and Harris Francis. "Anthropological Traditions Versus Navajo Traditions in Early Navajo History." In *Dine' Bikeyah: Papers in Honor of David M. Brugge.* Meliha S. Duran and David T. Kirkpatrick, editors, pp. 143-151, Albuquerque, New Mexico: Archaeological Society of New Mexico: 24, 1998.

Kent, Susan. "Hogans, Sacred Circles and Symbols—The Navajo Use of Space." *Papers in Honor of Leland C. Wyman*, pp. 128-136, Santa Fe, New Mexico: Museum of New Mexico Press, 1982.

Kidder, Alfred V., and Samuel J. Guernsey, *Archaeological Explorations in Northeastern Arizona.* Bureau of American Ethnology Bulletin, no. 65. Washington: Smithsonian Institution, 1919.

Klah, Hasteen. *Navajo Creation Myth: The Story of the Emergence.* recorded by Mary C. Wheelwright, Navajo Religion Series, Volume 1, Santa Fe, New Mexico: Museum of Navajo Ceremonial Art, 1942.

Klah, Hasteen. *Hail Chant and Water Chant.* Recorded by Mary C. Wheelwright, Navajo Religion Series, Volume II, Santa Fe, New Mexico: Museum of Navajo Ceremonial Art, 1946.

Klah, Hasteen. *The Myth and Prayers of the Great Star Chant and The Myth of the Coyote Chant.* Recorded by Mary C. Wheelwright, Navajo Religion Series, Volume IV, Santa Fe, New Mexico: Museum of Navajo Ceremonial Art, 1956.

Kluckhohn, Clyde, and Leland C. Wyman. "An Introduction to Navaho Chant Practice." *American Anthropological Association Memoirs* 53, 1940.

Kluckhohn, Clyde, and Dorothea Leighton. *The Navaho.* Cambridge, Massachusetts: Harvard University Press, 1946.

Kluckhohn, Clyde, W.W. Hill, and Lucy W. Kluckholn. *Navaho Material Culture.* Cambridge, Massachusetts: Belknap Press of Harvard University Press, 1971.

Koenig, Seymour H. "Drawings of Nightway Sandpaintings in the Bush Collection." *Papers in Honor of Leland C. Wyman*, pp. 18-44, Santa Fe, New Mexico: Museum of New Mexico Press, 1982.

Luckert, Karl W. "Toward a Historical Perspective on Navajo Religion." *Papers in Honor of Leland C. Wyman*, pp. 187-196, Santa Fe, New Mexico: Museum of New Mexico Press, 1982.

Madrid, Roque. *The Navajos in 1705: Roque Madrid's Campaign Journal*. Edited, annotated, and translated by Rick Hendricks and John P. Wilson, Albuquerque, New Mexico: University of New Mexico Press.

Matthews, Washington. "The Basket Drum," *American Anthropologist* (os)7(2): 202-208, 1894..

Matthews, Washington. *The Night Chant—A Navajo Ceremony*. Originally published; New York: Knickerbocker Press, 1902. Salt Lake City: University of Utah Press, 1995.

McGreevy, Susan Brown. "The other weavers: Navajo basket makers and the Museum's collection." *Messenger*, Summer 4-6, 1993.

McGreevy, Susan Brown. "The Storytellers: Contemporary Navajo Basket Makers," In *Willow Stories—Utah Navajo Baskets*, edited by Carol A. Edison. Salt Lake: Utah Arts Council, 1996.

McPherson, Robert S. "A Brief History of the Utah Navajos," In *Willow Stories—Utah Navajo Baskets*, edited by Carol A. Edison. Salt Lake: Utah Arts Council, 1996.

McPherson, Robert S. *Sacred Land, Sacred View*. Salt Lake City, Utah: Brigham Young University Charles Redd Center for Western Studies, 1992.

Morris, Earl H., and Robert F. Burgh. *Anasazi Basketry Basket Maker II Though Pueblo III, A Study based on specimens from the San Juan River Country*. Washington D.C.: Carnegie Institution of Washington, 1941.

Oaks, M., and J. Campbell. *Where the Two Came to Their Father—A Navajo War Ceremonial*. New York, 1943.

Olin, Caroline B. "Four Mountain Top Way Sandpaintings of Sam Tilden." *Papers in Honor of Leland C. Wyman,* pp. 45-55, Santa Fe, New Mexico: Museum of New Mexico Press, 1982.

Parezo, Nancy J. "Navajo Sandpaintings: From Religious Act to Commercial Art." Ph.D. Dissertation, Department of Anthropology, University of Arizona, 1981.

Powers, Margaret A., and Byron P Johnson. In *Defensive Sites of Dinétah*. pp. 12-13 and 106-107, Albuquerque, New Mexico: Bureau of Land Management, Cultural Resources Series No. 2, 1987.

Reed, Paul F., and Lori Stephens Reed. "Reexamining Gobernador Polychrome: Toward a New Understanding of the Early Navajo Chronological Sequence in Northwestern New Mexico." In *The Archaeology of Navajo Origins*. Ronald H. Towner editor, pp. 83-108. Salt Lake City, Utah: University of Utah Press, 1996.

Reichard, Gladys A. *Navaho Religion: A Study of Symbolism.*Volume I, New York: Published for Bollingen Foundation Inc. by Pantheon Books Inc, 1950.

Reichard, Gladys A. *Navaho Religion: A Study of Symbolism.* Volume II, New York: Published for Bollingen Foundation Inc. by Pantheon Books Inc, 1950.

Reichard, Gladys A. *Navajo Medicine Man Sandpaintings*. New York: Dover Publications, Inc., 1977.

Roessel, Robert A. Jr. *Navajo Arts and Crafts*. Navajo Curriculum Center, Rough Rock Demonstration School, 1983.

Schaafsma, Curtis F. "Ethnic Identity and Protohistoric Archaeological Sites in Northwestern New Mexico: Implications for Reconstructions of Navajo and Ute History." In *The Archaeology of Navajo Origins.* Ronald H. Towner editor, pp. 19-69. Salt Lake City, Utah: University of Utah Press, 1996.

Schwarz, Maureen Trudelle. *Molded in the Image of Changing Woman.* Tucson: University of Arizona Press, 1997.

Simpson, Barry, and Steve Simpson. "Peggy and Yeis." *Tied to the Post,* Twin Rocks Trading Post website; www.twinrocks.com

Stevenson, James. "Ceremonial of Hasjelti Dailjis and Mythical Sand Painting of Navajo Indians." *Eighth Annual Report of the Bureau of Ethnology,* Washington: Government Printing Office, 1891.

Stewart, Omer C. *The Navajo Wedding Basket,* Museum Notes, vol. 10, no. 9. Flagstaff: Museum of Northern Arizona, 1938.

Towner, Ronald H., and Jeffery S. Dean. "Questions and Problems in Pre-Fort Sumner Navajo Archaeology." In *The Archaeology of Navajo Origins.* Ronald H. Towner editor, pp. 3-18. Salt Lake City, Utah: University of Utah Press, 1996.

Towner, Ronald H. "The Pueblita Phenomenon: A New Perspective on Post-Revolt Navajo Culture." In *The Archaeology of Navajo Origins.* Ronald H. Towner editor. pp 149-229. Salt Lake City, Utah: University of Utah Press, 1996.

Tschopik, Harry Jr. "Navajo Basketry." *American Anthropologist,* Vol. XLII, No. 3, July-September, 1940; *Navajo Pottery Making, Papers,* Peabody Museum, 1941.

Van Valkenburgh, Richard F. "A Short History of the Navajo People." 1938 Radio Series on Station KTGM, In *Navajo Indians III.* New York and London: Garland Publishing Inc., 1974.

Van Valkenburgh, Richard F. "Navajo Sacred Place." Clyde Kluckhohn editor. In *Navajo Indians III.* New York and London: Garland Publishing Inc., 1974.

Weltfish, Gene, "Prehistoric North American Basketry Techniques and Modern Distributions." *American Anthropologist.* 32:454-495.

Wheeler, Charles W., and Scott Wilcox, and David O. Ayers. "Material Correlates of Early Navajo Ceremonialism." In *The Archaeology of Navajo Origins.* Ronald H. Towner editor. pp. 231-252. Salt Lake City, Utah: University of Utah Press, 1996.

Whiteford, Andrew Hunter. *Southwestern Indian Basket: Their History and Their Makers.* Santa Fe: School of American Research Press, 1988.

Whiteford, Andrew Hunter. *Traditional Baskets of the Southern Paiutes.* In *Translating Tradition: Basketry Arts of the San Juan Paiute,* edited by Susan Brown McGreevy and Andrew Hunter Whiteford. Santa Fe, New Mexico: Wheelwright Museum of the American Indian, 1985.

Wyman, Leland C., and Clyde Kluckhohn. "Navaho Classification of Their Song Ceremonials." *American Anthropological Association Memoirs* 50, 1938.

Wyman, Leland C. *Blessingway* (with *Three Versions of the Myth Recorded and Translated from the Navajo by Father Berard Haile*). Tucson: University of Arizona Press, 1970a.

Wyman, Leland C. *The Mountainway of the Navajo* (with *a Myth of the Female Branch Recorded and Translated from the Navajo by Father Berard Haile, OFM*). Tucson, Arizona: University of Arizona Press.

Interviews

David P. McAllester interviewed by Charlotte Frisbie, 1979.

Wesley Thomas, interviewed by Maureen Trudelle Schwarz, November 12, 1994.

Flora Ashley, interviewed by Maureen Trudelle Schwarz in Tsaile, Arizona, 1997.

Allison Billy, interview by the author, February 19, 2001.

Evelyn Rock Cly and her children: Martina Cly, and Theodore Cly, Navajo basket artists, interview by the author, February 20, 2001.

Peggy Black, Navajo basket artist, interview by the author, February 28, 2001.

Evelyn Rock Cly and her children: Martina Cly, and Theodore Cly, Navajo basket artists, interview by the author, February 28, 2001.

Betty Yazzie, interview by the author, March 1, 2001.Etta Rock, interview by the author, March 6, 2001.

Molly Yellowman, interview by the author, March 7, 2001.

Mary Holiday Black and her daughter, Lorraine Black, interview by the author, March 9, 2001.

Peggy Black, interview by the author, March 9, 2001.

Betty Yazzie, interview by the author, March 12, 2001.

June Blackhorse, Navajo Medicine Man, March 20, 2001.

Amelia Yellowman and Allison Billy, interview by the author, March 20, 2001.

Jenelia Benally, interview by the author, March 20, 2001.

June Blackhorse, interview by the author, March 21, 2001.

Mary Holiday Black and her daughter, Lorraine Black, March 24, 2001.

Sara Stanley, Navajo Culture instructor—Monument Valley High School in Kayenta, Arizona, interview by the author, April 9, 2001.

Sara Stanley's students: Dustin Sullivan, Freda Cook, Brenlita Cly, Petronia Johnson, Angie Stanley, Beranda Bedonie, Andrea Singer, Tee Jai James, Crystal Begay, Abraham Black, and J.D. Kinlacheeny, interviews by the author, April 9, 2001.

John Holiday, Navajo Medicine Man, interview by the author, April 16, 2001.

John Torres, Curator, Museum of Indian Art and Culture—Santa Fe, New Mexico, interview by the author, May 14, 2001.

Russell Griswold, Pawnbroker and Trader, interview by the author, May 15, 2001.

John Torres, Curator, Museum of Indian Art and Culture—Santa Fe, New Mexico, interview by the author, August 19, 2001.

Felicia Loretto, Jemez pottery artist, interview by the author, September 30, 2001.

Steven Begay, program Manager for Traditional Culture Program, navajo Nation Historic Preservation Department in Window Rock, Arizona, interview by the author, April 11, 2002.

Ed Chamberlin, curator, Hubbell Trading Post National Historic Monument, interview by the author, January 15, 2003.

Geno Bahe, Navajo Culture Educator, Hubbell Trading Post National Historic Monument, interview by the author, January 15, 2003.

June Blackhorse, interview by the author, January 27, 2003.

June Blackhorse, interview by the author, February 4, 2003.

Jim Copeland, Archaeologist, Bureau of Land Management—Farmington, New Mexico, interview by the author, February 6, 2003.

Clarenda Begay, Curator, Navajo Tribal Museum—Window Rock, Arizona, interview by the author, February 12, 2003.

Rachel Miller, District Archaeologist, Jicarilla Ranger District, U.S. Forest Service, Bloomfield, New Mexico, interview by the author, February 14, 2003.

Clayton Long, Bilingual Coordinator, San Juan County School District—Blanding, Utah, interview by the author, May 1, 2003.

Jim Copeland, Archaeologist, Bureau of Land Management—Farmington, New Mexico, interview by the author, May 7, 2003.

Charlene Rock, Basket artist, interview by the author, May 7, 2003.

John Torres, Curator, Museum of Indian Art and Culture—Santa Fe, New Mexico, interview by the author, May 8, 2003.

Don Mose, Bilingual Curriculum Developer, San Juan County School District, interview by the author, October, 2003

Index

Collecting Authentic Indian Arts and Crafts

Traditional Work of the Southwest

Indian Arts & Crafts Association
and the Council for Indigenous
Arts & Culture
$16.95
1-57067-062-5
128 pages
7" x 10"
color photos

"A **valuable work** to own. . . .
In this book a team of experts has
created guidelines for learning to
identify quality, evaluate dealers,
ask questions, and recognize
fraudulent work."
   Cowboys and Indians magazine

Georgiana Kennedy Simpson, author of *Navajo Ceremonial Baskets*,
wrote the sections on rugs, baskets, and pottery in *Collecting
Authentic Indian Arts and Crafts.*

"**Well-designed** and **reader friendly,**
insightful publication."
   Today's Librarian

"**Good advice, indeed!**"
   The Indian Trader

"A **superbly presented** and **comprehensive resource** for collectors and
dealers of Native American art forms. A unique team of Native American
artists and art experts brought decades of experience and individual
research to the production of this authoritative reference, explaining the
dynamic history and technical processes of their crafts as well as their
personal views into their creative worlds."

Midwest Book Review

St. Louis Community College
at Meramec
LIBRARY